"Everyone should tap into this treasure of wellness. The book provides the quintessential path to healthy recovery from any of life's grief."

—Bill Genêt, Director, P.O.P.P.A.
Police Organization Providing Peer Assistance

"Gifts My Father Gave Me is a book of hope and inspiration. Sharon Knutson-Felix takes the reader on her life's journey and shares her powerful story of love, loss, and learning to live again after the devastating tragedies that struck her family. She demonstrates that life can be good again, even after profound loss.

—Patricia Loder, Executive Director
The Compassionate Friends

"We all need a little inspiration to pull us through a difficult time in our lives. Prepare to become immersed in Sharon's story and learn the secrets to finding joy."

—Craig Floyd, Chairman, N.L.E.O.M.F.
National Law Enforcement Officers Memorial Fund

Gifts
My Father Gave Me

Finding Joy After Tragedy

Sharon Knutson-Felix

with Allen R. Kates

HOLBROOK
Street Press

Published by
Holbrook Street Press, Tucson, Arizona USA

Publisher's Note
This is a true story. The name of only one individual has been changed: Deana. This book is designed to provide information in regard to the subject matter covered. It is sold with the understanding that the publisher and author are not engaged in rendering psychological, financial, legal, or other professional services. If expert assistance or counseling is needed, the services of a competent professional should be sought.

Gifts My Father Gave Me

Cover design by Off Madison Ave

Publisher's Cataloging-in-Publication
Knutson-Felix, Sharon.
    Gifts My Father Gave Me : finding joy after tragedy /
Sharon Knutson-Felix ; with Allen R. Kates.
    p. cm.
    LCCN 2005910115
    ISBN-13: 978-0-9668501-1-6   ISBN-10: 0-9668501-1-4

    1. Knutson-Felix, Sharon. 2. Grief. 3. Bereavement
--Psychological aspects. 4. Consolation. 5. Children--
Death--Psychological aspects. 6. Widows--United States
--Biography.   I. Kates, Allen R. II. Title.

BF575.G7K62 2006   155.9'37'092   QB105-600194

Dedicated to

Ricky and Doug

...and to all those
who have lost loved ones

Contents

Chapters (continued):

"You desire to know the art of living, my friend?

"It is contained in one phrase: Make use of suffering."

—Henri Frédéric Amiel

Foreword

*L*osing someone you love is the hardest thing most of us will ever have to endure. The grieving seems to go on and on and the pain is relentless.

Grieving is a natural, normal process that we all undergo after losing a loved one. What do I do now? How do I cope? How can my life go on? Will the pain ever end? These are some of the questions we inevitably ask ourselves during the grieving process, questions we think have no answers.

However, they do have answers if we allow ourselves to grieve and experience the full range of human emotions.

In *Gifts My Father Gave Me*, Sharon Knutson-Felix experiences the day all of us don't want to think about—the day her child is killed, and years later, the day her police officer husband is killed. But because of her upbringing, attitude, and faith, she gets through the grieving and the suffering and creates a new life for herself. She doesn't triumph over tragedy, because nobody can, but she endures it, she grieves, moves through her emotions, survives the loss, and finds happiness and joy afterwards.

How she went through the grief process and how she endeavored to heal is what the book is about. The book is intensely powerful, funny, sad, joyful, and inspiring, and it shows the daring to overcome, and the strength, character and persistence it takes to confront despair and summon faith. Sharon's compelling story will make you laugh and cry. It exposes the richness of spirit that can dwell in the most desolate places.

Gifts My Father Gave Me

Most of us don't know what happens when we grieve or what to do for someone who loses a loved one. At the end of her story, Sharon offers a *Grieving and Healing Guide* that explains in detail what the grief process is, what to expect, and how to try to heal from the experience. It tells those around you, your loved ones and friends, what your needs are and what to say and do to comfort you.

Sharon was the first person I asked to join me in New York City to help those impacted by the attack on the World Trade Center on September 11th, 2001. We had worked together previously for several years, helping those affected by profound tragedies, and I had watched her demonstrate resilience and passion for comforting the *walking wounded*, those who have served honorably in the public safety family—police, firefighters, emergency medical personnel, and their families.

Despite her own personal *ground zeros*, Sharon never hesitated to apply her skill, faith and compassion. Consequently, I knew she would be the perfect person to reach out to those who were devastated by the terrorist attacks. Inside, I also knew she would be a tremendous comfort and support for me. Being in hell on earth, I needed her.

As a psychologist and sworn police officer, I counsel public safety professionals who struggle with stress, face life and death situations and who, themselves, must grieve the losses a public safety career can bring. These professionals respond to horrific situations that most will never see. They help citizens who have been severely injured, assaulted, raped and robbed of hope.

Sharon has a unique understanding of those who serve and the daily challenges they face—as well as insight into anybody who has lost a loved one.

Through her handling of her own tragic losses, Sharon proves that we are not powerless in the face of adversity. She shows us how the cruelest life experiences may bring us bountiful gifts—grace, courage, hope and a strengthened spiritual life.

She shows us how the lessons her father taught her (*gifts my father gave me*) about forgiveness, compassion, generosity, kindness, faith, courage, peace and prayer gave her the strength to survive the pain and sorrow of her losses.

This book will touch your heart, give hope in your journey, help to deepen your faith, and give you the courage and awareness to find joy after tragedy. I pray that you will be enriched by *Gifts My Father Gave Me* in the way that I have been in my friendship and work with Sharon.

—Sarah J. Hallett, Ph.D.

Clinical Psychologist,
Police Officer, Oro Valley Police Department

Chapter 1

First Love

*T*his book begins with a love story...

I was sixteen, and about to start a 2,200 mile bicycle ride from Houston, Texas, to Winnipeg, Manitoba, with a bunch of strangers. Twenty-eight guys, eight girls. Thirty-one days.

Sleeping outdoors, exposed to the sun and the rain, riding a bike on bumpy, rutted country roads, trusting people I didn't know. Were my parents out of their minds? No, it was their idea.

We were living in Coffeyville, Kansas, and on Sunday, June 3rd, 1973, the day before departure, my mom drove me to Houston. She introduced me to the leaders of the bike expedition, and one of them said, "You're kinda outgoing, aren't you, Sharon?"

"I guess," I said.

"Why don't you get people to meet each other?" he said.

So I did, and went to meet my future husband. Talk about unintended consequences...

People were swimming in the pool and sunning. I said hello and we started talking. I rummaged around in my duffel bag for a hat, looked up and saw this guy standing there. He was exceptionally handsome, tall, thin, with dimples and good hair, a Tom Selleck actor type. I hadn't met him yet, and I sure wanted to.

He was changing his shirt, and I said, "Hey!"

He looked over at me and said, "Me?"

"Yeah," I said. "I can see you."

And he said, "Yeah...?" Like it's no big deal.

"Well, I don't want you changing clothes thinking nobody can see you," I said. He shrugged and rolled his eyes.

Mom, you can go home now, I thought. And she did.

Later that afternoon, we were taught how to disassemble and reassemble our bikes, and I saw this guy again. We were supplied with yellow 10-Speed Schwinn Continentals, and we stole a few glances while the leaders droned on about nuts, bolts, brake cables, and how to fix a flat. I thought, Surely, if I have a flat, out of twenty-eight guys, one will fix it for me. One guy in particular.

Even later, I saw this guy at *the Pickle*, a big green trailer that carried our food and camping supplies. Its sides opened up to numbered cubbyholes where we stuffed our belongings. My cubbyhole number was 11, and when I looked through the hole, I could see the other side, number 27, which belonged to the Tom Selleck look-alike. Lucky me. Lucky him.

Soon it was time for dinner in the park, a barbecue of ribs and chicken. Yummm... Unfortunately, this was June in Texas, a terrible month for bugs and humidity. The mosquitoes feasted on us while *Tom* and I waited in line, eyeing each other. After we got our food, we sat down to eat with other people. We didn't sit together, not yet. As gregarious as I was, I was feeling shy around him.

I was tired from traveling to the meet, and after dinner lay down on top of a picnic table. *Tom* wandered over and sat on a bench.

"Hey, I can see you," he said.

"Yeah, so?" I said.

"I don't want you changing clothes or anything."

We were off to a meaningful start, and once the clothes thing was out of the way, got down to serious talk. I discovered he was not Tom Selleck after all, but Doug Knutson from Moody, Texas, which is outside of Waco, and the oldest of five kids. I was the middle child, the oldest girl of five kids. His mom had gone to Bethany Nazarene College (the sponsor of the bike tour). My dad had too, and we had a connection. Doug had recently graduated from high school and said he was thinking about college.

Oh, boy. Lots of serious talk—church, school, parents, friends, music, everything I was *least* interested in at that moment. Besides his short, wavy, dark brown hair, I was most interested in his killer blue eyes.

I analyzed the competition. There were seven other girls, and they were busy with guys lined up three deep wanting to talk to them. They were too distracted to focus on Doug. We were a rumpled posse of girls. No makeup, no jewelry, and we wore the same clothes— sneakers, black shorts and a deep green nylon tee-shirt slashed with two gold bands across the front. Yet the odds for a date were with us no matter how we looked.

Doug and I talked late into the night, and when I said I lived in Coffeyville, Kansas, he started calling me *Coffeyville.* The next day everybody was calling me Coffeyville.

In case you are wondering, I was not thinking *husband.* I wasn't even thinking boyfriend. I was thinking, Oh, good, somebody to talk to. Sure, sure, tell me another one...

Gifts My Father Gave Me

The next morning, the first day of the trip, the director of the program arranged us in groups of six. Doug and I were not assigned together. That would not do.

During the first break, Doug pedaled up and found the way to my heart. He handed me a Diet Dr. Pepper, which I always drank, and a Snickers bar, which I loved. Close bonds are made of such things. After that, whoever arrived first bought whatever the other wanted.

After a few days, the director allowed us to choose our group, and we naturally chose each other's. From then on, Doug and I were together, and we got to know each other fast. Think about it. You get up in the morning, don't wash, don't put makeup on, get on your bike and take off. You are true to who you are. Because you can't ride seventy miles, day after day after day, sweat bullets, wear the same clothes for a month and pretend you're somebody you're not.

What Doug saw, dirty hair and all, was what he got. And since hygiene and grooming were not going to count for much, I had to let my sparkling personality and brilliant organizational skills attract him. I mean it. I think the main reason Doug and I became attached was because I knew how to organize *laundry...*

On the second night of the trip, I was washing clothes, and he acted helpless. With a sigh, I told him to give me his clothes, and then sorted them, washed them by color code, and folded them nice and neat. He made a big deal out of it and made me feel smart. I did his laundry from then on... What a fool I was.

Doug did things for me in return. He was strong, and when the peddling got tough, he grabbed the six-foot orange florescent flag attached to the front of the bike and dragged me along the road and up the hills. He dragged me up a lot of hills. Many more than he needed to.

I was attracted to him physically. After all, I was sixteen and hormones were raging like a stormy river. While riding, we told jokes, we laughed a lot. He sang *Wichita Lineman*. He loved John Denver, he knew every one of his songs. *Rocky Mountain High, Take Me Home, I'm Just A Country Boy...*

Doug was a country boy. He had to call home and didn't know how to place a third-party call. Must have been embarrassing for a girl to show him how to make a phone call, but he didn't let on.

He wasn't wearing a class ring, which was big in those days, everybody wore a class ring. I figured he had a girlfriend back home in Texas wearing it. I didn't say anything about my suspicions, and then when we got to a stop six days into the trip, ten letters were waiting for him. They smelled like perfume, and red lips were pressed on the back of the envelopes, as if somebody wearing lipstick had kissed them.

He said the letters were from his mom. Oh, sure... I thought, We'll have fun while we're out here, and then I'll go home and he'll go home, and that will be the end of it.

About a week into the trip, we stopped in a town, went swimming, and caroused at a snack bar, and this town girl came on to him. It was sickening, at least to me, and everybody teased him. She was like a drunken barfly. She told Doug she wanted him to go home with her, and everybody took sides.

Go with her...

No, don't go with her...

A little later, we went to an armory, and flung down our bedding in a circle, like in a wagon train. I went to the bathroom, washed my face and brushed my teeth. When I got back, I was surprised he was still there. Our sleeping bags were five or six feet apart, and he was lying on top of his.

Gifts My Father Gave Me

"Oh, I thought you were going home with Suzy," I said.

"Rules don't allow it," he said. A big grin grew on my face. Then he said, "Maybe I should have. She would have tucked me in."

"I guess you miss your mom, you know, the one who wrote those letters with the lips."

"Yeah, I do."

I glided over to his sleeping bag, told him to get in, and zipped the bag up to his chin. Real tight.

"Well, Coffeyville, my mom kisses me goodnight," he said.

I bent over to give him a peck on the cheek, and suddenly felt his hand behind my head. He pushed me toward him and held my lips to his. How he got his arm out of the bag is a mystery. After that, I didn't have to wait until bedtime to sneak a quick kiss or two or three...

The pace we kept during the trip was exhausting. We'd get up around five o'clock in the morning, mount our bikes by six, ride twenty or thirty miles, stop around eight or nine, eat breakfast, get back on the bikes, stop at noon for lunch, hop back on the bikes and try to get in early at our next stop. Most days we averaged sixty-five miles, but several days we rode ninety miles before dinner. Some days we traveled 100, and one day we did 107.

More than anything else, my bottom ached, and it hurt as bad on the last day as it did on the first. I'd splurged and bought nylon biker shorts. I thought they'd make a difference. They didn't, and I stuffed underwear and tee-shirts down the back of my shorts to try to ease the pain. Even they didn't work.

The best day was when we biked to a town and the town folks cooked for us. We were a big deal, like celebrities, and the police escorted us with flashing lights and wailing sirens, and everyone in town showed up.

In the smaller towns, the story of our trip was front page news. Local newspapers sent reporters to interview us, and the townspeople turned up to talk to us. Most of us didn't want to talk to anybody. We wanted to fall down and shut our eyes.

I always wanted to talk, Doug didn't. Sleep was his priority. The town often wanted to feed us. They'd put on barbecues, with hamburgers and chicken. Considering how tired we were, I'm surprised we didn't pass out with our faces in the potato salad.

The jaunt that sticks out in my mind as the toughest was the ninety mile ride from Manhattan to Sabetha, Kansas. It was 106 degrees and the wind rocked us, gusting to thirty miles per hour. The hills were long and steep and I counted every push on the pedals. Doug had left early with a guys group and wasn't there to help and encourage me. I was exhausted. I cried, the other girls cried, and even some of the boys cried. Hard to believe I worked at the Sonic drive-in for months to earn the $300 registration fee for this torture.

After fighting the wind into Sabetha, we wheeled over to the town armory. The community was ready for us with charcoal, smoke and chicken on the barbecue. I dismounted painfully, and, feeling too tired for food, trudged into the building. On the floor on top of my sleeping bag was Doug, passed out and snoring, and a photographer from the local newspaper was snapping his picture.

I woke him up and told him about the picture, but he said he'd bet a million bucks it didn't happen. I bet him a million it did. He said he'd come to Coffeyville to collect, and I bet him another million he wouldn't.

"You get home," I said, "and your girlfriend's there, and you'll say, 'Sharon, who?'"

Gifts My Father Gave Me

He said he didn't have a girlfriend, only a girl he dated some. "What about the ring?" I said. He claimed he had left his ring at home because he didn't want to mess it up on the trip. Really...

After a month pedaling the back roads of Texas, Oklahoma, Kansas, Missouri, Iowa, and Minnesota, we crossed into Canada. My parents and two sisters pulled into Winnipeg in our station wagon with a camper trailer attached to take me back. I asked dad if Doug and I could borrow the car to go into town for souvenirs. Doug drove. We ate lunch at a fine restaurant, and I had to pay for my own lunch. I thought, What a tightwad.

On the last night, everybody exchanged phone numbers and addresses. You know, "I'll write you, we'll visit." We knew we'd never see each other again.

The next morning, we were packing the station wagon, and Doug was about to get on the bus to take him home. I suddenly realized... Gee, I've been with this guy for thirty-one days and now I'm not going to see him anymore. We gave each other a hug, and I reached up to kiss him goodbye. He said, "Your dad is looking."

I didn't care, for it was at that moment I knew I loved him. I knew his heart, and couldn't imagine life without him.

Then he got on the bus and I got in the car, and we drove down the road. He went one way, I went another way, and that was the end. I was bawling my eyes out, and my mom said, "You'll never see him again. Get over it."

I knew she was right. I just didn't want her *saying* it.

Chapter 2

The Visit

*W*e drove back following much the same route as the bike trip, and when we stopped in Sabetha, Kansas, on the front page of the June 21, 1973, edition of the *The Sabetha Herald* was a story about our bicycle trip, and, as I predicted, a picture of Doug snoozing. The article began:

> Sabetha was invaded at mid-afternoon Monday by a group of uniformed flag-flying bicyclists...

The story sounded like the D-Day invasion of Normandy. Under a picture of Doug stretched out on my sleeping bag, his hands across his stomach, the article said:

> It's not all fun and games as this young rider indicates. He simply passed out on the armory floor...

I mailed his parents the picture to forward to him in Oklahoma City where he had moved to attend college. And wrote:

Gifts My Father Gave Me

> Dear Mr. and Mrs. Knutson:
> I was your son's maid, and did his laundry. He was asleep and didn't know this picture was being taken.
> Yours truly,
> Sharon Rushing

In Doug's note, I wrote:

> I won the first bet. Who will win the second?
> Love, Coffeyville
> (P.S. I do miss you.)

A couple of weeks after I got home, a letter from Doug arrived. He asked me to call with my phone number because he didn't want to owe me a million dollars and was coming to Coffeyville on Friday. I'd already given him my number, which he had probably lost. My parents didn't let me call guys, but I called anyway.

"I'm breaking a rule and calling you," I said, "but that's only to remind you I won the bet. Are you really coming to Coffeyville?" I said, trying to act disinterested by yawning like a bored debutante at her coming out party. He assured me he was.

I think you will appreciate how excited I was not only because I adored Doug, but also because for a teenager Coffeyville was boring. Dreary. Mind-numbingly dull. It's an old town close to a river that often overflows its banks. The streets are paved with red bricks and the biggest thing that ever happened while I lived there was the opening of a Wal-Mart store. I hoped Doug's visit would break the monotony and calm.

I waited for Doug all day Friday. He didn't show, and I got angry. Early Saturday morning he phoned and said he was sorry, he had to work late last night.

"You could have called," I said. "You're such a jerk."

He said he was coming today and would be here by noon. He was in Oklahoma City and I was in Coffeyville, 180 miles away, about a three hour drive. I was so happy my cheeks were burning.

He didn't show up, and I got mad again. My mom wanted me to go to the store with her, and I didn't want to leave. My brother Bill teased me, saying, "He's not coming, he's not coming..." and I got mad at my brother. And my mom was mad at me because I wouldn't leave the house. Everybody got mad at everybody, but finally I gave up waiting and went shopping.

When I got home, Bill was on the phone and said some guy wanted to talk to me. It was Doug and I yelled at him for standing me up a second time. Once I let him get a word in, he said he'd totaled his car in Collinsville, Oklahoma.

I told him to stay there and I'd get him. It's like an hour and a half drive. I hung up, and ran out to the car. My mom was unloading groceries, and I said, "I've got to go to Collinsville, Doug wrecked his car."

My mom decided she'd better go with me, and we got in the car. "Where is he?" she said.

"Somewhere in Collinsville," I said.

"Well, where?"

"Maybe at the hospital." Then it occurred to me I didn't ask him where he was or if he was okay.

"How're you gonna find him?" she said.

Gifts My Father Gave Me

"We'll go to the police station and ask them."

"Ask them what? What kind of car does he drive?"

"I don't know." I didn't ask him that either. I didn't ask him anything.

"Typical sixteen-year-old," she said.

We got to Collinsville and on the outskirts saw a junkyard. A car with its front smashed in was sitting at the curb. It had Texas plates. We got out and peered into the car. It was messy, had to be Doug's. It was locked and nobody was around.

I was dying to go to the bathroom. We shot into town and pulled into the first gas station. And there was Doug standing out front. I immediately jumped out of the car, hugged him and forgot to go to the bathroom.

"Your mother's looking," he said.

I didn't care. I wanted the world to see. I asked if he was okay. Then we went back to his car, and got his stuff. Apparently, he'd rear-ended somebody who stopped in front of him unexpectedly. Then he had his car towed to the junkyard and sold it for $25.

Years later, he said he'd spent so much money trying to see me, he had to marry me.

We brought Doug back to our house, and my dad asked if the car was still running. My dad was pastoring a church in Coffeyville, but was a good mechanic.

"I don't know," Doug said.

"Well, Monday I'm taking you back to Collinsville and we're going to look the car over," he said. Twenty-five dollars was way too cheap.

On Monday, we drove to the junkyard, and my dad told Doug to tell the guy his dad won't let him sell the car. The guy didn't mind, and we hauled it back to my house. My dad said the motor looked fine and they should pull it out and put it in another vehicle. Doug wondered how you would do that. He wasn't mechanical at all. He hadn't even changed the oil in a car. Heck, he hardly knew how to run a lawnmower. As it turned out, Doug's father Jean had a Chevy truck that needed a motor.

Doug hopped the bus to Texas, got the Chevy truck and drove it back to my place. My dad got the engine hoist out and told Doug what to loosen and to remember where all the pieces went, and the two of them lifted the old engine out. Doug had never done anything like this before. They dropped Doug's engine in Jean's truck and my dad told Doug how to hook it up. Doug said he thought, I'll never put this back together. But it ran and Doug couldn't believe, even with my dad's supervision, that he'd hooked everything up himself.

The day we hauled Doug's wrecked car to our house, my brother Bill had his motorcycle dismantled in a gazillion pieces in the middle of the garage. By the next weekend, Bill had reassembled it and then rode it. Doug was amazed. He'd never seen people like us.

After that, he visited every weekend and worked on the truck. My mom loved him. He was polite, respectful and always happy. We did everything together. He got involved with the teen group at my church, and became part of our family. As Doug's college classes hadn't started yet, the weekends were ours.

Soon everyday was ours.

Chapter 3

The Ring

About six weeks after Doug's first visit, we went to pick up my class ring at the jewelry store.

"You want to get an engagement ring?" Doug said.

"Oh, sure," I said. I thought he was hilarious.

I tried on several engagement rings, assuming it was a joke. Then he said, "Which one do you like?"

"I like the first one I tried on," I said.

He asked the clerk how much it was, and then whipped a checkbook out of his back pocket, wrote out the check and handed me the ring. We hadn't talked about getting engaged or even going steady. We certainly hadn't talked about getting married.

After we got home from the store, I said to my dad, "You want to see my class ring?" I held out my finger with the engagement ring on it.

He examined it and said, "Is it a prize from a Cracker Jack box?"

"Da-ad! It's an engagement ring."

"Oh," he said.

Then we showed it to my mom. Her reaction was a little more dramatic.

"You're too young to get engaged," she shouted.

Gifts My Father Gave Me

She ranted and raved, and said I had to finish high school. Doug was scared. He'd never seen my mother apoplectic. I told him it was my dad he should be afraid of.

Three months later, in November, we decided to talk to my dad. *Seriously* talk to my dad. I told Doug my dad was always in his office after services on Sunday, and predicted what he would say.

"He'll say we're too young, this is not the wisest thing to do. He won't say *No* because I had cousins who ran away and got married and my dad told me he never wanted me to do that."

Doug and I waited until everybody left church, and then went to see him. I said, "Dad, Doug wants to talk to you," which I'm not sure are the words the father of an adolescent girl wants to hear.

I left. I didn't want to witness his reaction. As I skedaddled out the door, Doug looked at me with wide, panicking eyes. Then it was Doug and my dad and an empty silence.

"We want to get married, right away," Doug told my father.

"You're too young. It's not the wisest thing to do. Why don't you wait?" my dad said.

Doug was shocked that my dad said exactly what I said he'd say. Doug took a deep breath. "I want to marry your daughter now."

"Now...?"

"In January." Three months away.

"You have to make me one promise," my dad replied, staring him in the eye, evoking fear you'd experience on a runaway train about to jump the track. "You won't move from Coffeyville until Sharon graduates from high school."

"Okay," Doug said.

I think Doug would have agreed to anything.

At lunch time, we were sitting around the table and almost done eating and my dad said, "Well, I guess Doug and Sharon are getting married in January."

You'd think he'd announced we were joining a cult of devil worshippers. My mom threw her napkin down, kicked her chair back, and said, "Over my dead body..."

She stomped into the bedroom and slammed the door. My dad went after her. Doug looked like he was about to throw up. I got up and started the dishes. I heard my mom crying and my dad saying, "Well, Dicksie..."

I couldn't hear everything, but I did hear her say, "Are you an idiot, Andrew? She's sixteen-years-old!"

Soon my dad came out, patted me on the back and said, "She'll be okay." I kept doing the dishes.

A couple days later, my mom knocked on my bedroom door. She reminded me that I had an opportunity to go to Switzerland with the church group. I was on the district Bible quiz team, but if I got married, I wouldn't be allowed to go.

"Don't give that up," she said. Then she bargained with me. "If you wait on getting married and go to Switzerland," she said, "then we'll pay for your whole wedding."

Wow. Bribery usually worked. It was tempting. "No, I'd rather get married," I said.

"You'll be married the rest of your life. Don't you want to go to college?"

"I just want to get married," I said.

"Then you'll pay for the wedding yourself," she said, "and don't even think of inviting anyone in my family."

In case I missed the point, she added, "I will not put my name on a ridiculous invitation where people think I approve of a sixteen-year-old getting married."

"You were fifteen when you got married," I said.

Gifts My Father Gave Me

Wrong thing to say. She slapped me across the face. That was the only time in my life I wanted to hit my mom back. I bit my lip, and said, "Dad said I could get married, and I'm getting married."

"What about being a missionary?" my mom said. I'd told my parents I wanted to serve people in other countries and spread the gospel. "Are you going to give that up, too?"

"Getting married doesn't mean I can't be a missionary," I fired back.

After that exchange, we didn't speak for awhile.

Doug went home and told his parents. They were not pleased. "You're only nineteen, you're too young..." Same stuff.

His dad got out a pen and proved to him on paper that on his salary from a part-time job, we couldn't live. That wasn't a big issue to me because my family had never had enough money to live on but somehow managed. Forget the reality check, I had an answer for everything.

Desperate to stop Doug from ruining his life, his parents said they thought I was a wild kid because I went places most kids my age didn't go, and did things most kids my age didn't do, (like ride 2,200 miles on a bicycle trip with their son), and perhaps Doug should reconsider who he was marrying. Wild? Me? The preacher's daughter? Come on...

Doug was dealing with his parents' objections, and I was dealing with my mother. My dad's mom was living with us then, and she liked Doug. "Dicksie's a little high-strung," she said. "She'll come round. Don't worry."

I didn't worry. My mom and I ignored each other, and that worked for me. I carried on as if everything was normal. After school one day, I went to the printer and brought the big invitation book home and set it on the kitchen table. I wrote up the order like I was going to purchase cartoon invitations, something silly, and I knew my mother would object.

Sure enough, she protested. "Why would you order something like that?"

I wanted to say, What do you care what I order? But I wasn't disrespectful to my mother. Not verbally.

She leafed through the book and said, "Why don't you pick out something nice like this..." And she chose my wedding invitations. I ordered them and put her name on them. Be that as it may, we still hadn't made peace, and weren't talking.

Next came the dress. I had to go shopping for material to make it, and since I wasn't speaking to my mom, I asked my grandmother to write a note to get me out of school. My mom overheard the conversation and said, "Where are you going?"

"To Tulsa," I said.

"What are you going to get?"

"Some material."

"What kind of material?" she said.

"I don't know. When I see it, I'll know it." I was thinking, You're not talking to me, leave me alone.

"I think I better go with you," she said. "Pick me up after school."

My mom and I went to the store, and if not for her, I wouldn't have gotten anything done. I became frustrated. I had no idea what I wanted. Mom was a seamstress, and knew exactly what I needed. Because of her, we came home with enough material for my wedding dress and the bridesmaids' dresses. By the end of the day, my mom and I were friends, and we were talking again. Then, with her blessing, I sent out invitations to our family and friends, including her family, who she'd told me not to think about inviting.

Doug and I didn't have much money so my parents paid for the wedding reception, and I paid for the dress material, invitations, cake, and flowers. Doug's parents paid for the tuxedos and rehearsal breakfast. What we put our parents through. My poor mom.

Doug and I got married on January 12th, 1974, and six inches of sleet and ice coated the road. Breakfast and dress rehearsal were at 6 AM, and we got married at ten o'clock on a Saturday morning. All our relatives came, and it was a big, beautiful wedding. Because I was underage, my dad signed papers that allowed me to get married. Doug was old enough and didn't need his parents' permission. My dad officiated at the nuptials, Doug's father Jean gave the invocation, and my brother Bill walked me down the aisle.

The *Coffeyville Journal* was there to record every breathtaking detail and the article in the newspaper the next day gushed like a nineteenth century romance novel:

> The (bride's) gown was of Victorian style with high collar, scalloped lace, and Juliet sleeves. Her sweeping train was of pastel scalloped ribbon lace. Her elbow-length tiered veil of bridal illusion was held by a scalloped Camelot headpiece trimmed in pearls.

Great, huh? I could have been Scarlett O'Hara in a scene from *Gone With The Wind*.

Before Doug slipped the ring on my finger, he turned to me and sang a verse from the song, *More*. I responded with the next verse, and then we finished the song together in harmony. You've probably attended weddings where the bride and groom sang and you wanted to hide under the pew. Well, Doug and I were good. We were stupendously good. We could have won first place on the TV show *American Idol.*

My brother Ande, who lived in Oklahoma City, brought the bikes we used on the trip, numbers 11 and 27, to the church. We were going to ride them down the road and out of town, but the roads were too slick. Instead, my dad got up at 4 AM the morning of the wedding and shoveled in front of the church. The newspaper took a picture of us riding away on the sidewalk.

Pedaling along the sidewalk and smiling for the camera, it never occurred to me that marriage was more than a bicycle ride to *happily ever after.* Doug and I had never talked about what being married meant.

I know I was excited about cleaning my own house, not my mom's house, my house. Who wouldn't be, right? I was excited about fixing my own dinners, and went to the grocery store and bought those little mayonnaise and mustard jars and the one-time sugars instead of the ten-pound bags. Everything cost twice as much, but I didn't know that. I was excited because I had my own dishes and pots and pans, my own kitchen, my own refrigerator.

Doug and I had never discussed having kids. We'd never talked about what we wanted to do in life. We were young, and got married and didn't have a clue. The thing we had in common, though, was our upbringing. Since childhood, we were taught to live for the Lord. My dad often said, "Would you do it for God?" and that affirmation became part of my life and our common ground.

Our life together had a goal or theme, that our lives would be how we were raised. Our lives would serve people.

Chapter 4

A Married Woman

We moved six blocks from my parents' place, and rented a house for $105 a month. It was white clapboard with two bedrooms, and it was small, 900 square feet. The bathroom had an old fashioned claw foot tub, and the living room and kitchen were tiny.

The front porch was big enough for only one person to sit on it at a time, and if you weren't careful, you could fall off into the bushes. It's a good thing we didn't drink.

The owners lived next door, and once a week the guy came over with his Black Flag sprayer, and like a big game hunter with an elephant gun chased the roaches around the house, bellowing "skeet, skeet, skeet..."

I don't know why he felt he had to converse with the roaches, but the critters were a definite low point at the beginning of our marriage. The wedding gifts were a high. Among the many presents were about fifteen sets of sheets. I changed the bed every night, and slipping into a fresh bed and pulling the sheet up to my chin was pure joy.

Saying I was without a clue about marriage is likely an overstatement. I knew how to keep a house, I knew how to cook. My mother taught me well. Like her, I loved to entertain, and instead of my friends dropping by my mom and dad's house, now they were coming to my house. I was playing house and having fun.

School, on the other hand, was a pain. I'd promised my father I'd finish high school, but the school messed up my records and the principal said I couldn't graduate. I think I was more upset about my dad's disappointment than about whether I would graduate or not. Finally, my father stepped in, proved I had enough credits, and I received my diploma in the mail. It was too late for the prom, not that I cared—I was a married woman.

Church was the other part of my life. A big part. Shortly before I graduated from Coffeyville High School, the Sunday School superintendent announced they were looking for a second and third year Sunday School teacher. I had a passion for church, especially for helping kids, and went to see him. I was all set to be patted on the head and taken immediately to my classroom of smiling faces. Instead I got a shocker.

"You will never teach a class in my Sunday School," the superintendent said.

"Why not?" I said.

"Your dresses are too short."

This was the seventies, the era of the miniskirt, but I came from a conservative home and did not wear short dresses. Maybe shorter than his wife, who was in her mid forties, which was very old to me at the time. She wore dresses below her knees and a net on her head. I guess compared to her, I was a Jezebel and should have been strutting the back alleys of London or Paris. Okay, to be fair, my dresses were well above my knees, but not as short as a miniskirt.

I was annoyed at the superintendent's narrow view. However, I loved going to church. That was more important than teaching. Then one day I wanted to sing a solo piece I really loved in front of the congregation. The superintendent's wife said, "No."

Flabbergasted, I asked why. She said I was up front too much. I guess she would have preferred that I wore a dress down to my toes and hid my hair under a scarf. I mean, I had a pure heart. I didn't get up there to show off. It wasn't an ego thing.

I gave up on the singing too, but as each Sunday came and went, the Sunday School episode festered in my mind. I was not asking to run heavy machinery. All I wanted to do was teach Sunday School.

I went to see my dad, and said the superintendent was basing my skill and knowledge on how long my skirt was. My dad said, "This is between you and the superintendent. I'm not getting in the middle of it."

Well, I was ticked off at my dad. He was the pastor, he should stick up for me. After I got home, I talked Doug into going with me to confront the superintendent. I phoned and asked if we could come over after church on Sunday night, and have a talk. And a talk we had.

"What is the problem?" I said.

"You know what the problem is," he said.

"Why can't I teach?"

"Your dresses are too short."

"My dresses are not too short. This is your issue."

"Look, you're popular, and kids like you. They'll want to grow up and be like you."

"What's wrong with that?" I said. I was a good person, a role model.

"You have too much influence over them."

That was the dumbest thing I'd ever heard. "I don't understand," I said, "are you physically attracted to me?"

Gifts My Father Gave Me

It was out of my mouth before I could stop it. Boy, I had a lot of nerve. To my relief, Doug broke into the conversation. "I don't get it. Why would you want to hurt Sharon?"

You have to give the superintendent credit. He didn't get huffy and throw us out. He took our confrontation in his stride.

Before we left, I said, "I think we need to pray because I have a bad attitude. I need the Lord to help me, and you need His help too."

We prayed. It didn't help.

We left and for days I seethed about the situation. I told my dad about the meeting. My dad said, "You know, when people get between you and God, they're closer to God than you are."

I was allowing the superintendent to interfere in my relationship with God. I was the one who wouldn't change her skirt so I could teach Sunday School. I was the one who wasn't singing God's praises in church. My dad didn't let us blame other people for things. If you have a problem, it's your problem, not somebody else's. "Nobody can make you a problem unless you allow them to," he told me many times.

He was right, but that was beside the point. How about a little sympathy here, dad? Stick up for your daughter. If I had not been his daughter, if I'd been anybody else in the church, I think my dad would have stood up for me. But instead of fighting my battles, my dad wanted me to work out my own problems. At my age, I wasn't good at it.

One night soon after I was forbidden to sing, I was in church and the superintendent said something, I don't even remember what it was anymore, and I stomped out of church thinking he was the meanest person in the world.

A Married Woman

Doug was working nights driving a mail truck to Kansas City, and I was alone. I went to sleep and had a dream...

> *People in the streets are running around and shouting, "The Lord's coming back. God's coming back to earth..."*

> *I look up in the sky, and see a golden honeycomb, an enormous bee honeycomb with hexagonal holes descending from the sky. It draws near the ground and everybody scurries about looking for a hole that their body fits into. Then they crawl into their hole and lie there.*

> *I try to find my hole and I can't find it. Nothing fits. I'm desperate, crying, running and running, and whenever I see an empty hole, I throw myself in, and either can't get in because it's too small, or I get in and fall out because it's not my shape. It doesn't fit me. It's not my hole.*

> *Then the honeycomb lifts off. As it rises, I try to grab on with my fingertips, but it is slightly out of reach, and I know it's heading back up into heaven, and I'll be left behind.*

> *As it climbs into the blue sky, I see the superintendent and his wife, and they're stretched out in their holes and waving goodbye.*

Gifts My Father Gave Me

I woke up in a cold sweat, and prayed aloud, "Oh, God, please... I don't want to be left behind. Help me have a good attitude. Help me forgive them."

As a result of the dream, I acknowledged that I had become obsessed with their judgment of me. I had become unforgiving and hateful, and couldn't go to church and worship God anymore because of my anger towards them. Bitterness was like a thorn in my flesh, and my anger controlled me. It possessed me. And my spirit was becoming a desolate place, a desert with no tree to shade me from the hot sun.

I had to do something about this, and invited the superintendent and his wife to our house. They graciously accepted. I cooked dinner for them and they seemed impressed that somebody my age could keep a beautiful home and was capable of fixing a great meal.

I told them about my dream, and said, "I want to apologize for my attitude. I still don't understand what your problem is with me, but I know what my problem is. I have become bitter and unforgiving, and hope you will forgive me."

I thought they would feel sorry and ask me to teach. They didn't. But I wasn't bitter anymore.

You know, this is what gets me about God. He should have made the superintendent apologize, but that's between the superintendent and God. I can't ask God to influence somebody else. I can only ask God about myself, and it was enough that He made me aware of my attitude and removed bitterness from my heart.

I've often asked God, "Lord, why are you always on my case? Why don't you straighten out other people who have issues?" I'll never figure that one out. When I go to heaven someday, I'll ask Him about it.

By then I probably won't care.

Chapter 5

Pregnant, At Last

When I turned eighteen, I told the doctor, "I'm never going to get pregnant."

"You're young, don't worry about it," he said.

"There has to be something wrong," I said. "We've been married more than a year."

I wanted kids. At least a dozen. To me, that's what life was about, having kids and family. 'Cause when I grew up we had a big family, five kids, and it was fun. Five was good, twelve had to be better.

I hoped the doctor was right, and went home and waited for life to begin. I picked up my sisters and took them to school. I waited... I went to junior college in a two year program, and I waited... I worked at two part-time jobs: baby-sitting and as a freight company billing clerk, starting at noon, staying until the trucks left around six, sometimes not until nine.

Waiting was like trying to stay awake for the Tooth Fairy. You believed it would come, wondered if it was real, but you awoke the next morning to find a coin under the pillow. If only getting pregnant was that easy and all I had to do was leave out a tooth.

Gifts My Father Gave Me

Doug said he wasn't worried, but I think he was anxious, too. And, like me, he went through the motions of living while we waited for new life to announce itself.

He went to college. He felt an obligation because his mom and dad were teachers and his dad was a school principal. But Doug didn't like it, and didn't finish the first semester. Then he worked for the county driving a dump truck. He made $320 a month, not a high paying job, but a good job for a kid who didn't go to college. On weekends and sometimes at night he worked at a gas station. My father was always remodeling something and Doug helped him for extra money.

Doug eventually left the county and went to work for a private mail service on the night shift. He picked up mail in Coffeyville and all the stops on the way to Kansas City and back. I usually got off before he went to work and he would often be home before I went to school the next day. We didn't see each other a lot, but we had our whole lives ahead of us, and we knew things would get better.

Finally, the Tooth Fairy arrived. A year and a half after we were married, I became pregnant. We were euphoric. Then several months later, the Waco, Texas, church that Doug had grown up in offered us jobs as youth directors. Doug had been involved in the youth group, and I was always a leader at my church. I think they were looking for people who would love the kids, get along with the pastor, and do the job for next to nothing. We were available, and cheap.

About a month before I was to give birth, we trucked our belongings and furniture to Doug's parents' house in Moody, Texas, and stored them there until we could move. We had to stay in Coffeyville because our health insurance was only good for Kansas, and moved in with my mom and dad to wait for the baby.

Pregnant, At Last

It was a Wednesday night, and the girls and my mom had gone to church. Doug and my brother Bill were outside working on a van. They did van conversions: carpeting, paneling, beds, windows, you name it.

I went outside and said, "We should go to the hospital. I think I'm going to have the baby."

"Right now?" said Doug.

"Not this second, but soon."

"We have to finish this up. Can't you wait?" said Doug. "I'll take you in a bit."

Somebody was waiting for the van and Doug wanted to get paid for the work. I went back in and waited. We had gone to *Lamaze* classes and knew the baby could take awhile. By the time my parents got home from church, I was hurting. About an hour later, my mom went out to talk to Doug.

"Doug, you've got to take Sharon to the hospital. She's in labor."

"Okay, okay," said Doug.

As my water hadn't broken, there seemed no reason to panic.

"Her contractions are getting stronger," said my mom.

Around ten at night, Doug took me to the hospital, and the nurse agreed I was in labor. Back then they did horrible things to prep you, like give you an enema. After that ordeal, Doug and I tried the breathing stuff we'd learned. I was huffing and puffing like a marathon runner when my dad arrived.

He told Doug they should "let Sharon rest." I got mad because they were going to leave, but my dad had been through five births. He knew about the waiting. "Let's go for coffee," he said, "she'll be here when we get back."

Very funny.

Gifts My Father Gave Me

Doug returned an hour later and nothing had changed. I was achy and miserable. Hours passed, it was early in the morning and Doug was tired. The doctor arrived and checked me.

"You're fully dilated," he said, "I'm going to break your water. That should speed things along."

He broke my water, and I was ready.

"I gotta push," I yelled.

"No, no, not yet," said the doctor.

"I'm having the baby..." I said, and it hurt. "Give me a spinal."

I'd discussed this with Doug before, but it was my choice. I was the one in pain. I was the one who wanted to clobber whoever touched me.

"Sit up with your feet on the table," said the doctor.

I did.

"Put your legs up, and wrap your arms around your legs."

I did. Then I had another contraction, and felt the baby's head poke out.

"I need the shot," I shouted.

The doctor brought the needle to the table.

"I'm giving it to you in the spine. You have to be still," he said.

"Hurry up, hurry up!" I screamed.

I saw the color leave Doug's face. The doctor was poised to stick a gargantuan needle in my back, and Doug was afraid it would paralyze or kill me. Doug touched the side of my face with his fingers and said, "Please be still." Then he wrapped his arms around me and held me. The doctor jabbed me with the needle.

I waited for relief from the pain... Nothing happened. It didn't work. And the pressure from the baby trying to get out was unbearable.

"Mom... mom..." I wailed.

My mother wasn't even at the hospital. When Doug told her later I cried out for her, she said, "Why was she yelling for me? I'da slapped her and told her to shut up."

After having almost half a dozen kids, she had little patience for cry babies.

To heck with the spinal. I lay down and the baby popped out, and I felt instant relief. He was a big guy, weighing 8 pounds 12 ounces, and Doug was happy it was a boy. He kissed me, went home and went to bed. He was exhausted.

I was exhausted, too, but couldn't sleep. I was too excited about having the baby. We named him after Doug's cousin who at age sixteen was killed in a car crash. Later, this proved to be an immense irony. My new son's name was—

—Ricky Dale Knutson.

It was April, 1976, and life was wonderful. I had everything I always wanted.

When Ricky was six weeks old, we moved to Waco, Texas, about a ten hour drive from Coffeyville, Kansas. My parents were sad when we left. Often parents' biggest dreams are what degrees their kids will get, what college they'll attend. You read books and books about people who knew when they were two years old that they'd go to their parents' schools and graduate with honors and be an attorney.

That wasn't my dad's dream for us. He measured success differently. He didn't care how much money we would make. His dream was that whatever we did, wherever we went, we stayed faithful to the Lord, served Him, and served people. And that was our intent, and our passion.

In Waco, I worked full-time at the church for about $40 a week, and Doug, as well as working at the church, had a full-time construction job assembling metal buildings.

Doug's mom Betty helped me with Ricky and was a total caregiver. She loved babies, cuddled Ricky, helped me feed him and change his diapers. Despite that, I was tired all the time and felt overwhelmed. All of a sudden I had a baby and it took twice as long to get ready for work or anything. I was always late and in a hurry.

But the inconvenience, the exhaustion, the effort were worth it. Ricky was a beautiful baby with a happy personality. He had light brown, curly hair, light wisps of eyebrows, long dark eyelashes, and his face could go in an instant from a bashful, chubby-cheeked grin to a serious pensive stare. Everybody loved him, and wanted to hold him. When he was two, people in church took him places, like the zoo, to show him off. I can't count the number of times people said they wanted to keep him.

He was a respectful child. If you gave Ricky a piece of gum, he thanked you, and said "Yes, ma'am" and "No ma'am," and it was like you gave him the best thing in the world. He was well behaved, and everybody loved to do things for him. Usually, the more you give kids, the more spoiled they become. Not Ricky. He always acted grateful. I'd like to say it was because I was the perfect mom, but some kids are born with a disposition to be kind.

In Waco, we rented an apartment, and then Doug's parents moved to Oklahoma, and we moved into their house. We thought things were looking up, but from that point on, our financial and personal problems worsened.

The house was in the country about thirty-five to forty miles from town over a gravel road, and we felt isolated. I wanted to work outside the church, but there weren't any opportunities. Then Doug got sick. Both he and Ricky had to go to the doctor regularly and we no longer had insurance.

It turned out that Doug's wisdom teeth were impacted, and all four had to be cut out. We owed the dentist $1,000, a horrendous amount, and still owed our family doctor. I charged groceries at the local store and owed them about $400. After six months in Texas, income from our jobs did not cover our expenses.

During that time, my mom and dad moved from Coffeyville to Olathe, Kansas, and dad became the physical plant director of their church college. Dad preached on weekends and substituted for pastors who were away, but otherwise no longer pastored a church. I called and told him our situation. He offered Doug a job in construction at the college and said he'd pay for our move to Olathe. Needless to say, we accepted this unexpected rescue.

To save money, we moved in with my parents. They were building a house in Springhill, which was about twenty miles from town. They built the garage first with a small kitchen and bathroom that allowed them to live there while finishing the house.

They weren't expecting two more adults and a child, and it was close quarters, but they didn't complain and it became quite cozy. I didn't mind living in a garage. It was a roof over our heads and it was fixed up with curtains and paint. You really couldn't visualize that cars would soon be parked there and trash cans pushed against the back wall.

Because we were heavily in debt, Doug and I decided to get two jobs—*each*. In the daytime, I worked at an electronics company in the shipping department and Thursday to Sunday I waitressed the night shift at Denny's. Doug worked construction during the day and security during the evening at the college. My mom looked after Ricky, picking him up from the sitter's after she got off work, feeding him dinner, bathing him and putting him to bed.

When we slept, which wasn't often, it was on a twin-size mattress on top of a carpet remnant covering the cement floor. We had a gas heater, and in the middle of the night it often ran out of gas.

Driving home from work was a challenge, especially in winter. We had a used Ford Pinto, you know, the so-called exploding car, and the car slid on the ice, and shook and shimmied up and down hills. The heat didn't work and we had no money to fix it. I'd get home at night and my feet were like ice. I would scramble into bed and make Doug sit on them until feeling came back.

In an absurd way, living this poor was fun. We were young. It was an adventure. We were in it together, and I think it strengthened our bond with my parents and with each other.

But you only want to do it once in a lifetime.

Chapter 6

Pregnant, Again

Ricky was an easy baby to care for, and working two jobs, we soon got out of debt and moved into an apartment in town. Life was improving. Then I had Justin.

He was born in February of 1978, but, unlike Ricky, he was not born happy and healthy, and we thought he was going to die. He cried nearly every minute of every day and night. The doctors wrote on his hospital charts—

Failure to thrive.—

They said he might have cystic fibrosis. They said he might have a lot of things, but they didn't know. He had frequent infections and fevers, and they tested him incessantly.

After I brought him home, nothing changed. At night, I pulled a pillow over my head and cried along with him. Doug got up and took care of him. To get away from Justin's crying, I got a job on the switchboard at the college. I hired a babysitter, and a few weeks later, she called me at work and said she couldn't do it anymore. She said Justin should be in a hospital. I took off work and picked him up. He cried all night long, and I thought, My gosh, my life is ruined.

Seeing my plight, my best friend, Carol Sands, the wife of Doug's childhood friend Ron interceded and said she'd keep him for awhile. She was the only person Justin tolerated. When she rocked him in her arms, he stopped crying. Most of the time. But she had to pay him a lot of attention.

It was six weeks of peace and I caught up on my sleep. Then she called and said I had to pick him up, it was too much for her. When I got there, I saw that she'd broken out in hives.

"I'm sorry, Sharon, I can't do it," she said. "He cries all the time."

I put Justin and Ricky in the front seat of the car. They didn't have child seats then. Ricky stood beside me and Justin sat beside him. I set off for home, and, suddenly, a car stopped in front of us. I nearly didn't see it through my fog of tears, and slammed on the brakes. I threw my arm out and caught Ricky, but Justin fell on his face on the floor. He was screaming, and I sat there thinking, I want to leave him there.

When we got home, I picked Justin up and shook him and told him to quit crying. I put him in his room and shut the door because I thought I was going to shake him to death. Ricky turned on the TV very loud, which he was not allowed to do, and I spanked him. He was only trying to cope. He didn't want to hear Justin cry either.

I called my mom. Doug was there helping my dad build his house and was up on the roof. "I want Doug to come home," I said.

"What's wrong?"

"I hate Justin," I said, sobbing. "I wish I never had him."

Pregnant, Again

"I'm not getting Doug," my mother said. "You go eat something right now."

Picture this. I'm sitting at the kitchen table crying hysterically and saying I'm going to kill my baby and she tells me to eat something. But she wasn't wrong. A month and a half earlier I had gone on a liquid diet that was popular in the seventies. Nobody told us people were going nuts and dying from it.

I hung up the phone, and it rang right away. It was Doug's mom and dad calling, and I told them what was going on.

"Dad and I will drive up and get Justin," she said. This was unusual. Doug's mom and dad rarely did anything spur of the moment. They lived in Oklahoma City and drove six hours to our house in Olathe.

As soon as they arrived, they asked where Justin was. I said, "In his room," and Doug's mom packed his stuff, and they left. During their brief visit, I didn't say a word. I sat on the couch, dazed, and understood why people abuse their children. Because until you have experienced it, you don't realize how lonely it is to be a mom, handling kids all day, and at night not getting any sleep. I was not a bad person. I had reached the end of my ability to deal with the screaming, and if you have a sick child, I can see how you could become an abuser.

On Sunday, I was relieved that Justin was gone, and we went to church. Ricky was with us, and it was wonderful. The next day, I went to work and then to the doctor for a checkup and some tests. Doug had a vasectomy scheduled because I didn't want any more children, not after Justin. The doctor thought we were too young to make that decision, but I was insistent. I went back to work, and the nurse called me later.

"Congratulations, you're going to have a baby," she said.

Gifts My Father Gave Me

"I don't want to have a baby," I said.

"Maybe you should see the doctor," she said.

I didn't know what to do. I don't believe in abortion. I went to see the doctor and told him my dilemma. He felt better about the vasectomy now that I was pregnant, but when he found out I was on a liquid diet, he became annoyed and told me to get off it and eat something. Just like my mother. She could be a doctor.

The doctor said I was starving myself to death. The baby was taking everything I had and my body was out of balance. No wonder I was having emotional problems. He insisted that I start eating solid food and take vitamins to build myself up. After his evaluation, I felt a little better about my situation. But I still didn't want Justin back.

Four weeks later, we went to a family reunion in Texas. First, we drove to Oklahoma City to pick up Justin and Doug's parents. I sat in the backseat with Justin, Doug's mom, and Ricky. I hadn't seen Justin in a month. I didn't pick him up. I didn't hold him. Didn't change his diaper, didn't feed him. I ignored him.

At the family reunion, people said, "Oh, is that your baby?" Doug's mom Betty answered for me while she held and fussed over Justin and acted like he was hers. I didn't care. Justin was better off with her because she spent twenty-four hours a day taking care of him. She tried home remedies on him, and they had some effect. He certainly seemed to feel better. Maybe it was what the doctors had done. They had injected him with Cortisone and he had gained weight. He looked healthier. But I had no love for him.

When it was time to leave the reunion and go home, I refused to take Justin. He was only three-months-old, and I told Doug, "I don't want him back.

Your parents can raise him." Doug was angry with me and said his parents had their own lives to lead. But I left Justin in the car, and Doug's parents took him home with them.

The next Sunday, Doug had to go somewhere and I went to church by myself. There was a guest speaker from Britain preaching on the family. I sat there feeling guilty because I didn't love my son. I was a bad mom.

At the end of the service, the preacher asked if anybody wanted to pray at the altar, and I went down and kneeled, put my hands together, and closed my eyes. I prayed and bargained with God.

>—*I want to be a good mom, but don't make*
>*me take Justin back.*
>—*I'll take him back if you make him better.*
>—*I'll take him back, but I'm not going to*
>*quit my job.*

On Monday morning, I went to work. My face was puffy and my eyes swollen from crying. I was working in the financial aid office and my boss said, "You look like you've been beat up."

"I had a rough weekend," I said, and told him about Justin. And then I said something I swore I'd never say. "I need to give you notice. I'm gonna go get Justin and stay home with him. I can't work and take care of him."

I didn't know I was going to quit my job until that moment.

Two weeks later, we walked into Doug's parents' house and Justin was lying on a blanket in the living room. He was up on his hands and knees and had a big grin on his face, like he knew something. I picked him up and kissed him, and we took him home.

At night when Justin cried, I sat in the living room and held him. I rocked him and sang:

Gifts My Father Gave Me

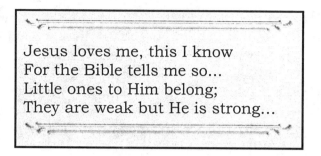

Jesus loves me, this I know
For the Bible tells me so...
Little ones to Him belong;
They are weak but He is strong...

I sang hymns and choruses of songs. Not once did I lose my temper or lose control. Isn't it remarkable that one week I refused to look at Justin and the next week I loved him? That I couldn't wait to get him home? That I had accepted I was going to care for a sick child? That I became willing to sit up nights, miss sleep, and be terribly tired?

I was pregnant, and yet being up all night rocking Justin became my most cherished time, when the house was quiet and it was me alone with my son. It wasn't that he was better. I was better. When I'd bargained with God, I said I wouldn't quit my job because the office was my safe haven, my place of sanity, but I knew in my heart I had to.

And when I did, peace filled my soul.

Chapter 7

Surgery

Still, everything seemed to revolve around Justin, even after I gave birth on Valentine's Day, 1979, to my daughter Misty, my little sunshine, who smiled every time she saw you.

I took Justin to the doctor week after week and told the doctor something was wrong. He said they'd tried everything, and suggested exploratory surgery. There had to be a reason for Justin's unending illness.

The night before surgery, a specialist came into Justin's hospital room. I was twenty-one, a kid myself, but doctors did not intimidate me.

"Why do you want your son to have surgery?" the specialist said in an accusatory voice.

"I don't want him to have surgery," I said. "I want him to be well."

"I checked him out in the nursery," said the doctor. "I examined his ears, nose and throat, and there's nothing wrong with him."

"I don't know who you are," I said. "I didn't ask you to look at my son. My son lives on Prednisone. Is that normal? That he should live on drugs? He's been in the hospital a dozen times, and he's only two. I have two other children and they're not like that. The day I took him from the hospital, he quit breathing and I had to revive him. The doctor in the emergency room said it was my imagination, that I was a nervous mother. I am not a nervous mother. It was not my imagination. He cries all day, everyday, and he's been sick since the day I had him. Don't tell me there's nothing wrong with him."

He got the message, and handed me papers to sign that gave them permission to fix anything they found wrong. The next morning, they took Justin in for surgery. The doctor said he should be out in an hour.

Two hours passed.

Three hours.

Then four.

Finally, they wheeled him out. The doctor said they'd inserted a syringe into his eardrum to draw fluid from his inner ear, and a huge amount of pus squirted out. To drain the infection, they'd implanted tubes in both ears.

The biggest discovery, however, was a nodule, a deformity, next to his vocal cords. The doctor said that fluid emanates from your lungs and you swallow it into your stomach, but because Justin's throat was small, the nodule caught the fluid. It didn't go into his stomach and instead remained in his throat, and the result was infection. Strep throat, tonsillitis, earaches.

The doctor was amazed Justin had not died. If he had, they would have called it *Sudden Infant Death Syndrome*—SIDS, which they knew little about. He said Justin survived because he was a fighter. When he lay down, he choked and gasped for air, and that's why I had to hold him up and rock him hundreds of nights in a rocking chair. Screaming and crying helped him expel the fluid and breathe.

The doctor didn't cut out the nodule, there wasn't enough of an opening to get at it. They treated him with steroids, and as he got older, his throat grew larger, but the nodule stayed the same size, and he didn't have to cry to breathe anymore.

I had my son back, and life once again became joyful.

Chapter 8

The Letter

A year after I had Misty, Doug stopped attending church. In addition to his job at the college, he had taken on a part-time job at a carpet store that kept him away some evenings during the week and most weekends. He was working all the time and said he needed time to relax.

I wanted him to go to church with me and the kids. We argued, and there was a lot of tension, but I didn't think the arguments were significant. Although we weren't seeing much of each other, I thought we were happy.

He didn't want me to work because he wanted me home when he got home. I needed to get out of the house, and thought, You take care of three kids all day and see how it is. So I worked occasional evenings, and once in awhile when I called home, he would be on the phone, or I would walk in and he'd hang up the phone. It was odd, but I didn't think anything of it.

At Christmas, Doug announced he was going to spend the holidays with his family in Oklahoma City. He didn't say *we* were going. Only he was going. He gave no explanation. I didn't know what to say, and he drove off without me and the kids.

Gifts My Father Gave Me

After I informed my dad about Doug, my dad came over and asked what was going on. I told him about the many hours Doug spent working, his time away from home, and the arguments. My dad said he didn't think the kids and I should spend Christmas without Doug, and believed Doug's parents felt the same way. He gave me money and a car and told me to go. I listened to my father, and when we pulled up in the driveway at Doug's parents' place, Doug didn't act happy to see us. He seemed preoccupied and distant.

After we got home, we argued again. This time about what we were doing on New Year's Day. We were feeling the stress of everything: hospital bills, Justin's illness, and never having much time for each other. On New Year's Day, I took the kids to my parents'. Doug didn't want to go. He said he was going for a haircut. The girl that ran the carpet store had promised to cut his hair. On New Year's Day.

When he got back, I said, "What's the deal with you and her?"

"What are you paranoid about?" he replied.

He changed the subject and accused me of wanting to go to my parents' all the time. All of a sudden, he didn't like my family. He said he wanted to do something different once in awhile, *like get a haircut on New Year's Day.*

A couple of days later, I needed money, and opened his wallet. Some newspaper clippings fell out, about eight of them. They were from a comic strip called *Love Is*, and showed funny-looking naked couples acting out romantic ideas and the captions were about togetherness, passion, tenderness, and sex. I thought I was going to throw up and was afraid of what these idiotic cartoons might imply. When he got home, I confronted him.

He told me a story about how the carpet store girl's husband had beaten her, she was going through a divorce, and he'd tried to help her. When I pressed him, he admitted he'd kissed her, that was all. I believed him. Maybe it was self-delusion, but Doug and I were always trying to help other people, and although we were constantly squabbling, we still had a good, intimate sex life, and a committed relationship. Again, he blamed our problems on my family. "Fine," I said, "then let's move."

We talked all night, we didn't sleep, and became close like we used to be. We decided to move to Dallas, where my brother Ande lived. I would move first and get a job and as soon as I had one, Doug would quit his job, move with the kids, and he'd look for work.

I called my brother, and he set up job interviews for both of us. Then things took a different turn. Doug had befriended Steve Bailey, one of the kids at the college, and when his parents visited, we invited his family over for dinner. Unexpectedly, Steve's father offered Doug a job in New Mexico working for him at a rural gas company. The job was driving a truck delivering propane in Broadview, a little town in the middle of nowhere. Doug flew out there and accepted the job. That put an end to our Dallas plans, and we couldn't be happier.

Doug moved on his own first. I had things to do. I had to paint the townhouse to ready it for sale, and my sister Terrie was getting married. After the wedding, the kids and I were going to join him.

One day I was going to see my parents. The kids were at Carol's place, and I put my niece in the car, grabbed the mail that had just arrived, and headed over to the college. I usually opened all the mail, no matter who it was addressed to. As I drove, I saw a letter addressed to Doug from the carpet store girl, and opened it. There were three pages. She said how she missed him and described the things they'd done together, sexually explicit things.

I don't know how I was able to drive after that. The windshield was a swirl of tears. But I got to the college, entered my dad's office and asked his secretary where he was. She said he was in a meeting with a group of people. I left my niece with his secretary, opened the door and barged in.

"Dad, I've got to talk to you," I pleaded.

Everybody stood up and left. I handed him the letter. He read it, and then my mom came in, read the letter and tears welled in her eyes.

"I'm not defending Doug," my dad said, "but it's understandable how this could happen."

"How...?"

"Doug works a lot," he said, "and when he goes home, there are three kids, and a lot of pressure and responsibility. He's a good-looking guy, people are after him to do things. He drives a little four-door Toyota and this girl has a sports car and is free and has money. She needed him, he was her rescuer, and it's obvious she wrote this letter for you to read. There's too much detail. And you don't even know if it's true."

How could my dad be logical when I couldn't think straight?

"This is not something you can solve over the phone," my dad said. "Doug has to come home or you have to go to New Mexico."

"Where's she getting the money to fly there?" my mom said. My mother was always practical.

"Put it on American Express," said my dad.

"Who's going to look after her kids?" said my mom, and they got into an argument.

When Justin was in the hospital, I often got home late and everyday on my front porch was a plate of homemade bread. This was a gift from Reneé, a friend who worked at the college part-time. Even though it's inexpensive to make, it's not the bread, it's the time, effort, and loving kindness behind it. I called her and told her I had to go to New Mexico and would she watch my kids.

"Who's taking you to the airport?"

"Mom and dad, but they're arguing about putting it on their credit card."

"How much is the ticket?"

"Three hundred and five dollars."

"I'll bring you the money," she said.

Reneé picked me up at my parents' office and took me home. I packed a bag, and on the way to the airport, I described what the letter said. Then she told me a story about her parents. She said her parents grew up in the church, and were leaders. A church member was having problems. Her husband had left her and she was sick, and Reneé's dad went over to repair things in her house. They became involved, and everybody in the church knew about it.

We drove down the road, and Reneé described her parents' miserable lives. They left the church work they'd loved, and it took them a long time to go back. What Reneé's dad did was wrong, and he was sorry and repented. He was willing to do anything her mother wanted to make things right, but her mother would not forgive him. And he wouldn't forgive himself. Reneé didn't want Doug and me to fall into that trap.

Before Reneé picked me up, my dad reminded me of the church service we had attended before Doug left for New Mexico. An evangelist was speaking that day about families and relationships, and at the end of the service, he said, "Take your spouse by the hand, look him in the eye, and ask 'Is it well with your soul?'"

Gifts My Father Gave Me

Doug and I were holding hands and I noticed he didn't look at me. There were lines around his eyes and he appeared troubled. The preacher said that if something is not well with your life, come down to the altar and pray. Doug let go of my hand and stepped down the aisle to the altar. After church, I said, "Are you okay?"

"Yeah, I am now," he said.

"Do you want to talk about it?"

"Not right now," he said.

My father was in church that day, and didn't say anything until this moment.

"Doug was dealing with the Lord about something, and the Lord forgave him," my dad said. "If God forgave him, can you forgive him? Because if you can't, there's no reason for you to go. And if you do forgive him, you can never bring this up again. You can never hold it over his head."

My dad wasn't admonishing me. He was sharing from his heart. He was saying, "Do what's right, not what you feel like doing."

After talking to my dad, I called Doug to say I was flying out to see him.

"Why are you coming?" he said.

"I'll tell you when I get there," I said, weeping.

He knew. He didn't know about the letter, but he knew that somehow I knew everything.

When Reneé dropped me off at the airport, she gave me money for the ticket and said not to worry about paying her back. She said the Lord had blessed her family. She hugged me and said while I was gone she would pray for me. Maybe the Lord had blessed her, but He had also blessed me with a kindhearted friend.

I bought a book for the flight to take my mind off the mess I felt my life had become. It was *Kramer Vs. Kramer.* I didn't know it was a book about divorce and child custody. I sat on the plane and read and sobbed into a hanky. The flight attendant asked if I was okay. I held up the book. She saw the cover, nodded and said she'd read it. I'm sure she thought I was reacting to the story.

I got up, squeezed down the aisle and into the bathroom, threw up, and had diarrhea. We landed in Lubbock, Texas, and I switched planes to a puddle jumper that held twelve people. You couldn't stand up straight without banging your head. And it had no bathroom!

Chapter 9

Lies

I flew from Lubbock to Clovis, New Mexico, and had a horrendous headache. I hadn't eaten all day. My face was swollen from crying. I was a disaster.

We landed, and taxied in. I could see a car parked near the terminal and Doug was standing beside it. He had to borrow a car to pick me up, and my first thought was, He is so good-looking. I love him.

My shoes clicked down the metal ramp, and I glided toward him and into his arms. I felt our cheeks wet with tears. When he let me go, I gave him the letter right there on the tarmac at the entrance to the terminal, in front of people getting off the plane.

We got in the car and he turned on the light and read it. He said, "I begged God you would never find out."

"You lied to me!"

One minute I'm happy to see him, I'm madly in love, and the next minute I hate his guts—he's the worst person in the world, I'm getting a divorce, put me back on the plane, I'm going home, I don't know why I flew out here.

Gifts My Father Gave Me

He started up the car and we drove out of the airport. "Everything in the letter is true," he said. "Except I never said I loved her."

"You sent her flowers on our anniversary," I said. "On our anniversary!"

Finally, I understood the whole picture. When Justin was in the hospital, I sat by his bedside, and when Doug finished work, he took my place and I went home to take care of Ricky and Misty. What I didn't know until this letter was that after I went home, Doug left Justin alone and went to her place.

"You spent all those nights with her when I thought you were at the hospital looking after Justin."

We sat in silence for awhile. Doug was staying at his new boss's house in Broadview, and said we should let them know I made it. "Do you want dinner," he asked.

"I can't eat," I said. No kidding.

We arrived at the house, and Leroy and Betty Bailey saw the state I was in. They hugged me and asked if they could do something to help.

"I screwed up," Doug interrupted. "I cheated on Sharon. I don't know why I did it." He started weeping, and then I felt sorry for him.

They prayed with us and asked the Lord to mend our hearts and help us find forgiveness. They gave Doug money to go home with me because they knew if he didn't go, I would never come back.

We flew back to Kansas the next day. By the time we'd arrived, I had calmed down and saw a clear direction. I told my parents I had forgiven Doug, and, as we had intended, we were moving to Broadview. We rented a U-Haul truck and our friends and family helped us load up. Reneé made sandwiches for everyone, and was pleased that I'd forgiven Doug. She didn't want to see a repeat of her parents' life.

We still had a few days for goodbyes, and made the rounds of our friends. We went to the hospital to see Carol who had had a baby. When Doug entered her room, she ignored him. She was angry for what he did to me. Her husband Ron put his arms around Doug and said, "We'll keep you in our prayers. We know you and Sharon can work this out."

That's when I got a bright idea. I asked Doug to talk to this woman and straighten her out, but he didn't want to see her. Instead, I wrote her a letter. I told her that, as she had planned, I read the letter she sent Doug. I said Doug's actions were hurtful, but we would survive. "He might have sent you flowers, but he doesn't love you. He loves me." I said dumb stuff.

On the day we were setting off, my mother said goodbye. She wouldn't cry in front of us. She doesn't like to show emotion. She thought I was dim-witted anyhow for moving out there with three kids. When I tried to talk to her about the move, she refused to discuss it. My dad hugged me and said, "Sharon, the Lord can give you strength to do anything. He can forgive sin, and He can help you to forgive. I'm proud of you."

We pulled out. I was in the Toyota, and Doug drove the U-Haul pulling our little truck, and I saw tears running down my dad's face. I cried for hours on the road to New Mexico.

My father told me years later that as he watched us drive away he felt awful seeing his grandkids go off to another state because he wanted to be there for us, he wanted to protect us and help take care of us. He saw us going away with the person that hurt not only me but all of us. He also said he wanted to seize Doug by the throat and pulverize him for hurting his daughter. But he knew we were doing the right thing.

When we left for New Mexico, it was winter and frigid outside, and so was my heart. One night, I would

Gifts My Father Gave Me

want Doug to love me, the next night I didn't want him in the room with me. "I can't stand you, I hate you, don't touch me"—I said. My feelings were all over the place. After a couple of weeks, however, things were better between us. I felt we had a good chance of getting past this, and I settled into my new surroundings.

We lived in an old stucco house that had been painted white many years before. The color had faded, and in splotches now resembled dirty black soot. It was a rural community and our closest neighbor was two miles away. Our water came from a well, and the biggest attraction as far as Ricky was concerned was mice. Lots of mice. Thousands of mice. Ricky liked to make the rounds of the mouse traps, pluck them up by the tails, and chase me around the house waving them like gruesome victory flags.

The house had three bedrooms carpeted in green shag (yuck), one bathroom (for the five of us), antique appliances in the kitchen (they should have been issued historic license plates), and a screened-in back porch where the washer and dryer wobbled and trembled during their frequent heavy loads.

The basement was unfinished and mirthless. We were told it was a good place to store canned goods, but there was no way I was going down the stairs to get food. It was the source for varmints including Ricky's mice, rats and poisonous rattlesnakes. I'd just as soon starve to death.

During the summer when temperatures soared beyond 100 degrees most days, the great outdoors spawned more mice, more rattlesnakes, fist-size hairy tarantulas, murderous black widows, and lots of cuddly black-tailed jackrabbits that loped around the treeless countryside.

The road was gray gravel, we had no green grass, just sunburned dirt, and most of what we heard all day was silence—except for the banging of the washer and dryer, and sometimes cars grinding by, and the bawling of ten Hereford calves with white faces and big blue eyes that gamboled in the pasture across the road. Ricky and Justin wore cowboy boots and chaps and with some effort rolled hay bales for the calves from our yard across the gravel road to the water tank.

It was windy all the time, and dust storms blasted through the cracks in the doors and window frames into the kitchen cabinets and hung in the air of every room in the house. Everything was dirty. When it rained, the road washed out.

That was my life in Broadview, New Mexico. Varmints, dust, dirt, wind, rain, and heat. I hated it. At the same time, we were a family, and that made it tolerable.

Then a package arrived in the mail addressed to me. Inside were letters and cards Doug had written to the carpet store woman, everything he'd ever given her. They said cloying things like:

I love you."
"Can't wait to see you."

I put the kids in the car and drove to Doug's workplace. I asked Betty Bailey where Doug was. She said he was out on a route delivering gas, and I said, "The kids and I are leaving."

"Why?" she said.

"He lied to me again. I've given up everything for him, and I have rights."

"Sometimes we have to give up our rights," she said. "You've got three beautiful children. Don't leave. Don't do this to your kids."

Gifts My Father Gave Me

She said she'd call Doug and give him the rest of the day off. She would look after the kids while Doug and I talked.

Doug and I fought all night. He said he was going to drive the truck off a cliff and kill himself. He was going to get the gun and blow his head off. I got the gun and said, "Go ahead, kill yourself. I don't care. I want you dead." Very mature of me.

We cried all night. We screamed all night. When I couldn't cry anymore, I ranted about how he had lied to me again. I bombarded him with questions like bombs raining down on a city:

"How can I ever trust you," I screamed.
"What does she have that I didn't have?"
"What was it like to make love to her?"
"What things did you do with her?"
"Did you take showers together?"
"What does she do for you that I don't do?"

Doug said over and over again, "Please Sharon, don't ask me... I don't want to remember." Maybe he didn't want to remember, but I wanted to know. I wanted all the details to rub his face in.

By morning, we were both exhausted, and I agreed that I would *try* to forgive him. I locked the package of letters and lies in a cabinet, and thought, If I decide to divorce him, I might need them for evidence.

I stayed, and we tried again, everyday a test of who we were, everyday a trial of how we could live together and keep a family intact. Living where we did in New Mexico was hard on both of us. Doug worked long hours. I was stuck at home all day looking after three kids. We didn't have TV, we got one radio station and it reported the ups and downs of the stock market, which was hardly relevant to my life. But we studied the Bible together. We attended a small church and got involved in it. We didn't have anybody except each other, and had to learn to face our problems head on.

Friends and family back in Kansas wrote us long letters of encouragement and said they were praying for us. Sometimes we had visitors. Reneé spent a week, and then another good friend, Jan Batley, came out. Ricky had attended her Sunday School class and she and her husband used to take Ricky fishing. Ron and Carol visited, and then my mom and dad.

Although everyone was supportive, I felt alone. They praised Doug for dumping the bimbo, but nobody said, "Wow, Sharon, what a great person you are. He did that to you and you forgave him." Nobody acknowledged how hard it was for me or praised me for how hard I was trying.

I guess I had not truly forgiven him.

Chapter 10

Forgiveness

Doug's boss suggested that we go to family camp, a church event that ran five days.

I didn't want to go.

Then I decided I did want to go.

And then I didn't.

I bounced back and forth. Taking three kids was a chore, and even though I had resolved in my mind that no matter the pain I would stick out our marriage, I didn't want to go with Doug. I went anyway, with him, and on Friday night during services, the song evangelist stood up and sang:

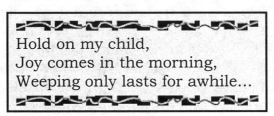

Hold on my child,
Joy comes in the morning,
Weeping only lasts for awhile...

That was all I needed to hear, and wept openly. They hadn't invited anybody to the altar, but I rose and stepped forward and knelt at the altar.

Gifts My Father Gave Me

I was brokenhearted, and asked the Lord:

Please help me to love Doug again.

Doug slipped down the aisle and knelt beside me. I prayed and asked the Lord to help me not dwell on how much he had hurt me and to help me forgive.

The five days passed, and instead of dread, I felt strengthened. We went home, and then, much to my surprise, had a fun weekend, and I realized that the Lord was willing to help me forgive him. But there was something in the way. It was me.

I went into the bedroom, unlocked the cabinet drawer, and stared at the hateful letters the girl had sent. In my mind, I heard the Lord say:

If you're going to forgive him, get rid of them.

I thought, No, I can't do that. Well, the Lord was not going to help until I did. Until I did, I would be bitter and cynical.

I gathered the letters, carried them outside to the trash barrel, dumped them in, struck a match and lit the edge of one of the letters. Once it was fully engulfed, I dropped it into the rest and watched them burn. After that I didn't feel the hurt and pain anymore. The knife sticking in my heart was gone, and the year we spent in New Mexico turned into a great period of our lives.

We still had problems. We took Justin to the hospital every other day for breathing treatments, and had no health insurance and mounting doctor bills, but Doug and I were still together and loving each other like couples do.

Chapter 11

Doctors

*D*oug's parents had moved to Phoenix, Arizona, and his dad was working for Aloe Vera Products running the production line. He called Doug and said there was a job opening supervising laborers, and they would pay $35,000 a year, which to us was a fortune. We moved right away.

A man from Monte Vista Church of the Nazarene rented us a house and the backyard butted right up to the church parking lot. On Sunday, we could walk to services.

We enrolled Ricky in the public school's kindergarten, and in February I was called to a parent-teacher conference. Ricky's teacher said Ricky had to repeat kindergarten. Repeat kindergarten? Who repeats kindergarten?

"Every paper he brings home has smiley faces and stars on it," I told her.

"Well, he is precious and adorable," she said, "I can't mark his paper wrong."

"You have got to be kidding," I said.

"He is the best behaved child I have ever met," she said. "But he doesn't know his ABCs, his alphabet. Everybody else knew how to count to 100 before they got here. Some of the children were reading."

Gifts My Father Gave Me

"That's why he goes to school," I said, "to learn this stuff."

"His verbal skills are on a fifth grade level, but that's not going to get him through."

Nobody told me my five-year-old had to be educated *before* he started kindergarten. I thought my job was to teach him social skills, and the school would do the rest. There was no *Sesame Street* on television then to teach him how to count.

We yanked Ricky out of public school and placed him in our church's private school. He was not a slow kid. It wasn't that he couldn't learn, he hadn't been taught. Nevertheless, with good instruction, by the end of the school year, he was ready for first grade.

I decided to send Ricky to attend first grade in the Christian school in Tempe where Doug's dad was the director and his mother was a kindergarten teacher. Justin was in preschool, and he could go too.

The arrangements were complicated. On Monday morning, I drove them to school. They went to their grandparents' home after school and stayed over Monday and Tuesday nights. I picked them up on Wednesday, and drove them back to school on Thursday. They spent Thursday night, I picked them up Friday after school, and they were home Friday, Saturday and Sunday. Then we did it all over again.

After a semester of this, it was too hard on them, and on me. At Christmas break, I was driving Ricky and Justin back from their grandparents and said, "Ricky, I don't like it when you guys are at grandma and grandpa's house. I want you home every night. I like to see you after school so you can tell me what you did. Would it make you sad if I changed your school again?"

"It's okay, mom. Whatever you want," said Ricky.

"You know you're not going to see your friends in Tempe anymore."

"I can make new friends," he said.

I whined and carried on, and he said, "Whatever school you and dad want me to go to is okay." I was more upset than he was.

I re-enrolled Ricky in the public school where he had flunked kindergarten. On the day I took him in, I brought his records to the principal's office, and the principal led us to Ricky's new classroom. Ricky didn't know anybody, but he marched in, big grin on his face, and waved to me. That was Ricky, good-natured.

The principal said, "That is the most handsome little lad I've ever seen."

Naturally I agreed. Ricky looked like Doug, and I dressed him to the tee, and parted his hair. He was the perfect child.

Justin was not the perfect child. It wasn't his fault, and since moving to Phoenix, he was better than he'd been, and getting better. But he still had relapses. I thought by now he should have grown out of the ear and throat problem. He was three, and he had fevers, difficulty swallowing, trouble breathing, and recurring sore throats and throat infections. I took a flashlight, pointed it down his throat and saw huge clumps hanging at the back on both sides. At that time everybody said, "Oh, you don't take tonsils out anymore."

My dad had a look and said, "You have got to get them out." I checked the Yellow Pages and found a pediatric specialist who was an ear, nose and throat doctor, and brought Justin in.

"What makes you think he needs his tonsils out?" the doctor said.

Before I could answer, he told Justin to open his mouth, and said, "Wow, those puppies have to come out." Justin's tonsils had swelled so big, they were restricting his breathing. The doctor examined his adenoids, which are up behind the nose, and they were infected too.

The doctor put Justin on antibiotics for ten days, and said he'd operate after the infection was gone. Ten days later, the infection was still there. The doctor put him on a stronger antibiotic. I told the doctor this was Justin's pattern. He doesn't get well.

Another ten days passed, and although Justin wasn't completely healed, the doctor gave the go-ahead. This was Friday and he scheduled the surgery for Monday.

A lot can happen in three days...

Saturday night we were having a special church service, and I made bread and one of my famous casseroles—a recipe I learned in Kansas that had chicken, wild rice, green chilies and a white sauce. Delicious. I told Ricky to take it to the preacher's house because the guest speaker was staying with him. Ricky stepped out the back door, tripped and fell, broke the casserole dish, dumped the dinner on the ground, and slit his wrist. I put a compress on the wound, and off we went to our new doctor.

Our doctor said Ricky had to see an orthopedic surgeon, and sent us to the hospital. In the emergency room, the orthopedic surgeon said a dish shard had cut into Ricky's tendons but had not severed them, and he would be fine. He sewed up his wrist and Ricky was brave and didn't cry too much.

That was Saturday.

On Sunday, we went to church, and friends Lois and Jim Severson invited us over after the service. Their daughter Amy was two like Misty, and they thought it would be fun for them to socialize. We sent all three of our kids home with Lois and Jim while Doug and I went to our place to change clothes.

Then we headed to their house, pulled up in the driveway, and were expecting a nice lunch. Their teenage daughter Debbie suddenly ran out of the house and said, "Something's happened to Misty. Mom and dad took her to Doctors Hospital."

"What happened?" I said, anxious.

"We don't know," she said.

We zipped down to 20th Street and Thomas, screeched to a stop, and rushed into the emergency room. There was Misty sitting on a chair, and Lois was holding a towel around my little girl's face. Both Jim and Lois were shaken and wide-eyed, and Misty's clothes were drenched in blood. I unwrapped the towel, and her face on one side was gone. I could see tissue and muscles hanging down. I couldn't see her eye.

"Do you know what happened?" I said, horrified.

"Debbie and I went outside and found her like this," said Lois.

The ER doctor called a plastic surgeon, and we sat down and waited. Misty was calm, hardly a peep out of her. Maybe she was in shock. The doctor was worried because her blood pressure was dangerously high, which usually doesn't happen in children.

I called Justin and Ricky. They were still at Lois' place, and I told them to look for what Misty cut herself on. We wanted to know what happened.

Then we waited some more. Two hours passed. Three, four, then five... The plastic surgeon didn't show up until five o'clock. He examined the open wound that was Misty's face. Then they strapped her on a papoose board with Velcro bands to prevent her from moving during surgery, and asked us to leave the room. She started to cry.

"If you're good," I said, tearfully, "after you're done we'll go get ice cream." I didn't know what else to say.

"The dog bit me," Misty blurted out.

"What dog?" I said.

"Amy's dog."

Gifts My Father Gave Me

A police officer at the hospital overheard this and accused us of trying to hide what happened. Can you believe that? He took a report and instructed Jim to quarantine the dog.

After the surgery, I was amazed at how good Misty looked. The doctor had restored her face, and her eye wasn't missing after all. The torn skin had covered it so it looked like it was gone. The doctor said only one nerve was nicked and he sewed that up too. Her face was swollen, that tiny face. It was the most beautiful face I'd ever seen.

Then the doctor said we could take Misty home. It was remarkable. After having her face sewn on, she didn't have to stay overnight in the hospital. We put her in the car and went to pick up Ricky and Justin. At Lois's house, Ricky said that while they were looking for what cut Misty, the dog bit him in the stomach.

That was Sunday.

Monday turned into a busy day. We took Ricky to Scottsdale Memorial Hospital for antibiotics for the dog bite. We took Misty to Doctors Hospital so the doctors could check her stitches. And took Justin to St. Joseph's to get his tonsils and adenoids out.

After Justin's operation, the doctor brought a jar with something disgusting in it into the waiting room.

"This poor child," said the doctor, displaying the jar. "Look at these adenoids. You can't even tell what they are. Your child has had severe infections and never got well because his adenoids were diseased."

That was a weekend I'll never forget. Misty recovered with a slender scar across her right cheek, but it's hardly noticeable. Ricky was fine, and Justin thrived. He stopped coughing and having fevers and gained weight. Why the doctor who put tubes in Justin's ears didn't take out his tonsils and adenoids, I'll never know.

In January, 1982, about four months after Justin had his tonsils out, a day I call *Black Friday*, the doorbell rang. It was six in the morning. Who rings your doorbell at six in the morning? It was Doug's boss. "The company is closing its doors," he said. "Don't come to work. You have no job."

It meant we had no health insurance. At least the kids' big medical bills had been covered, right? A week later, we received a letter from the insurance company denying our claims for Ricky, Misty and Justin. They said Aloe Vera had not paid its premiums for some time and we were not covered when we took the kids to the hospital. Now we were stuck with thousands of dollars in medical bills and Doug had no job.

With Doug's last check we paid off our car and a loan we took out to buy cattle in New Mexico, a venture we lost money on. We arranged to pay each hospital about $100 a month.

Doug opened a floor covering business. It was tough getting customers, and we only made about $7,500 that year and struggled to pay the rent and feed our kids. Then when summer came along, my dad invited Doug to return to the college in Kansas and re-carpet several buildings. We had no money—this was a gift.

For the next three months, we lived with my mom and dad while Doug worked. Doug made good money, and it gave us a start. After that, we returned to Phoenix and Doug resumed his floor covering business. My next door neighbor's brother-in-law was a rep for a grocery chain and he brought us broken boxes and dinged cans of food they couldn't sell. We lived on that for nearly a year. He even dropped off toilet paper that had been opened.

When Christmas came, we went to Oklahoma for Doug's sister's wedding. The boys were dressed in black suits with red cumber buns and red bow ties. Misty

Gifts My Father Gave Me

wore a red satin dress. It was a great wedding, but the joy of seeing my sister-in-law walk down the aisle was soon forgotten because a few days after I got home, I experienced every parent's nightmare.

Ricky was six-years-old...

Chapter 12

Jesus In My Room

*B*efore I take you on that agonizing journey, I'm first going to take you further back in time and tell you a story about Ricky when he was three, and we lived in Broadview, New Mexico...

One Sunday night, we got home from church and I put the boys to bed. They had bunk beds and shared a room. I kissed them goodnight, turned the light out, and went to bed. I was drifting off when I heard Ricky calling me. It was a frantic cry, "Mom, Mom, come here quick."

I got up and went to his room. "What's going on," I said.

"I'm scared," he said.

"Why are you scared?"

"There's something out there looking at me."

I looked out his window and saw nothing.

"Go to sleep, Ricky."

"Mom..."

"Close your eyes and turn your head away."

"Mom, I'm still scared."

I thought, Good grief, and picked him up. At three, he was kind of heavy. I got a flashlight and we went outside. Sitting on the well-house roof staring in his window was an owl.

"See," I said. He was happy it wasn't a monster. I took him back in and we went to bed. Before long, I heard the call again. "Mom..." And I returned to his room.

"I can't see the owl, I see those eyes and they're making me scared."

Living far out in the boondocks, we hadn't bothered with curtains, and couldn't shut out the staring eyes. Then I remembered what he'd told me that morning on the way home from church about his Bible verse in Sunday School.

"Hey Ricky," I said, "what was your Bible verse this morning?"

"When I'm afraid, I'll trust in the Lord."

"Let's pray and ask the Lord to help you trust Him so you can go to sleep."

"Okay..." he said.

I took his hand. "Jesus, will you be with Ricky and help him not be afraid?" He was asleep before I finished the prayer.

I went back to bed, snuggled up to Doug and told him about Ricky and the owl and how much he trusts Jesus. Next morning, we heard Ricky jump off the top bunk in his room and yell, "Mom, Dad, Mom, Dad..." and he ran into our room.

"What's up?" said Doug.

"Jesus was in my room last night."

"Really?" I said.

"Yeah, He really was. He talked to me."

I was nervous about this. He was telling me he was seeing things.

"What did He say," I asked.

Ricky crinkled up his nose and furrowed his eyebrows the way he always did when he was being witty or impish. "I can't remember, but He sure does love me a lot," he said.

The next time we had people over, Ricky couldn't hold back his joy in telling everybody that Jesus was in his bedroom and spoke to him. Then he asked a question only a kid could think of.

"Mom, if we die and go to heaven and we're with Jesus, why don't we die now? Because if we went to heaven, I could get wings and wear my bathing suit, and then if I wanted to swim I could fly down and swim in the pool. Then I could fly out and do anything I want to do."

"We don't want to be in a big hurry about this," I said, and had a good laugh. How do you answer a question like that?

For almost a year, Ricky told anyone who would listen about his conversation with Jesus. It was Ricky's favorite story, and it became more meaningful to me three years later.

Let's go there now...

*   *   *

Ricky is six-years-old. We had returned from Doug's sister's wedding. A few days later, I was feeling ill. It was Sunday night, and I was asleep. Ricky slipped into my room, tugged on the blanket and woke me. We had a waterbed, which was low, and he leaned over me, and said, "Mom..."

In the middle of the night, you don't want a kid bending over you. You don't know if he's about to throw up in your face. I pushed him back and crawled out of bed. Doug was asleep. He could sleep through anything.

Gifts My Father Gave Me

"Are you sick? Do you have to go to the bathroom?" I said.

"No."

I led Ricky into the living room. "What's wrong?"

"Mom, do you remember when we lived in Broadview?"

"Yeah."

"You remember I didn't have curtains on my window??

"Yeah."

"You remember that night Jesus spent the night with me?"

"Uh-huh."

"I keep thinking about that."

"How come?"

"I keep thinking about how much Jesus loves me."

We talked for awhile and then I asked if he was ready to go back to bed. I took him in and we prayed before he fell asleep. I woke Doug up and told him what Ricky said. I didn't know what to make of it. Why was he thinking about something that happened that long ago? Why was he fascinated with Jesus? Two days later, I understood. Ricky had given me a special gift, a blessing, and he wanted me to know everything would be okay.

The next day, a Monday, I went to the doctor, and he said I had pneumonia. He wanted me in the hospital. We couldn't afford it. He gave me a shot of antibiotic and decongestant, put me on a medicine and ordered me to stay home in bed or he would admit me to the hospital.

I was in bed the rest of Monday. On Tuesday morning, Doug got Ricky up, fixed pancakes for breakfast, drove him to school and went to work. I was lucky my sister Terrie was visiting from Kansas. She looked after my kids, as well as her own two. Then Terrie said she had to go to the store for Pampers for her son Dallis, who was asleep, and she asked me to listen if he woke up. She said she'd take Justin, Misty and her daughter Niki with her.

I'd been listening to a series of Bible study tapes, and I put one on the tape recorder. Among other things, the tape was about seeing God's strength and understanding His love. Before the sun set this day I would need both His strength and His love, because my life was about to change forever.

Chapter 13

Ricky

It rang and rang and rang. I didn't want to answer it. It couldn't be that important.

For a moment, it stopped ringing, it was quiet, and then the phone rang again, and I knew I'd get no rest if I didn't deal with it. I picked it up and croaked, "Hello."

A young boy was on the line. "Are you Justin's mom?" he said.

"Yes."

"Your sister wants you to come to 40th Street and Weldon. Your boy's been run over..."

"What...?"

I staggered out of bed, dizzy. I thought, I've got to find something to wear. I opened my closet door, and Misty, who'd just turned four, ran in from outside screaming. I thought she was with Terrie. She said something like, "Mommy, Justin's hurt. Justin's hurt! This lady wants to take you to Aunt Terrie."

There in my house, in my bedroom, was a woman I'd never seen before. I dressed quickly and called Carol across the street to look after the kids. I told her Justin was in an accident. I told Misty to get the pastor's wife, and hurried out the door.

Gifts My Father Gave Me

As I entered the stranger's car, I saw the children's pastor, Val Bolster, turning the corner in her car. She was taking her son Jeff to trumpet lessons. I flagged her down and asked her to follow me. She let Jeff off, and followed me to the accident scene.

When I got there, I saw an ambulance and paramedics. Terrie was standing beside a tree and she was screaming, "Sharon, *SHARON!*"

"Are you the mom?" said one of the paramedics.

"Yes. What..."

"Please, get in the ambulance."

The ambulance's doors were open, and Justin was lying on the gurney. His shoes and one sock were missing, and the other sock was halfway off. An oxygen mask was on his face and four people worked over him. I couldn't see him that well, and only caught a glimpse of his shirt. "If you want to go with us, then get in," said a paramedic.

I started to step up into the back when somebody said there was no room, and pushed me toward the front. I got in and the driver on the walkie-talkie said, "We're on our way..."

I turned around, and said, "Is he breathing?"

"No, ma'am," one of them said, "we're breathing for him."

I tried to catch my breath, but I couldn't. I thought my heart would burst and I'd never breathe again.

The tape I was listening to before I fell asleep was playing in my head.

This is a time to show you how much I love you...

"Did you say something?" said the driver.

"No," I said. "I didn't say anything." I must have spoken my thoughts out loud.

"Does he have any allergies?"

"Asthma. He's on medication."

God, please don't let him suffer anymore, I thought. He's suffered his whole life. If he's not going to have any quality of life...

"His birthday's tomorrow," I said.

After we got to Maricopa County Hospital, they pushed Justin's gurney through an open door into the ER and ushered me away toward a room. He was in their hands now.

Our children's pastor brought Terrie into the room. I was crying, she was wailing, and everyone thought she was the mom. Consequently, the ER doctor ignored me and updated her on Justin's condition. He said it didn't look good.

I needed Doug. He was out on a job somewhere and I hadn't paid attention when he told me early that morning where he was going. I called his parents who didn't live far from the hospital, and they said they'd be over right away. Then I called home and the pastor's daughter answered.

"Did Ricky get home from school okay?" I said.

"Ricky?" she said.

"Yeah. I left and he wasn't home from school."

She put her mother on the phone, and she asked where I was.

"The hospital... I'm checking to make sure Ricky got home from school," I said again.

"Sharon," said the pastor's wife, "Ricky's at the hospital. Justin's here in the backyard playing."

I didn't understand what she was saying. Terrie overheard me on the phone, and said, "Sharon, it's Ricky..."

"What?"

"Justin went to the end of the block with us, and decided he didn't want to go to the store. He turned around and went home. Ricky got off the school bus and saw us, and asked if he could walk with me and the girls."

Gifts My Father Gave Me

"Ricky?" I was confused.

"We were walking back from the store," she said. "Ricky was right behind me, and a car drove up on the sidewalk."

Reality slowly dawned on me. In my mind, I had lost one son, and now I had to face losing another. My mom always said that I liked Ricky best. At that moment, I knew it was not true. When I thought Justin was dead, and then Ricky, it was the same feeling. It was the same crushing, sickening feeling.

The bizarre things that go through your mind at a time like this. I thought, See, I don't love him more than the other kids. And then I thought, His birthday's not tomorrow, and he doesn't have allergies. I've got to tell them they have the wrong kid, because I told them he was going to be five tomorrow. It's Justin who's going to be five. Ricky's six, he's six...

Then I remembered seeing his shirt. Ricky and Justin wore the same clothes. From a distance, any mother could be mistaken. I asked the chaplain to get the doctor, but then the hospital supervisor and two doctors appeared. By now they had figured out I was the mom, and they had tears in their eyes.

"Mrs. Knutson, we're sorry," one of the doctors said. "Your boy didn't make it."

He only had on one sock, I thought. The impact from the car knocked him out of his boots, and he lost a sock.

"We tried everything. Kids have amazing little bodies, but after he was hit, he never breathed again. He didn't suffer."

They went on and on but I don't recall what they said. I know I heard his name. They knew his name.

—Ricky

I felt his name deep in my blood, and I wept uncontrollably. I didn't know I had that many tears in me.

Where was Doug...? I phoned my dad at his office. His secretary said he'd gone out of town to go camping for the weekend and didn't know how to reach him and my mom was off someplace. I told her about Ricky, and started to cry.

She looked out the window and saw my dad at the gas pump, and called him inside to the phone. My father said they'd leave Kansas immediately. My parents threw clothes into their bags, raced to the airport, and arrived as the plane was pulling away from the gate. Weeping, my mother told them why they had to be on that plane. They called the plane back, paid two people to get off, and let my parents board.

After speaking to my dad, I drifted out of the room. Our pastor, Lee Steele, had arrived earlier and I asked him if I could see Ricky. He left to find out, and then Doug's parents arrived. I told them Ricky was dead. Doug's mom gasped, and his dad sucked in air like he was going to faint.

My pastor returned with the hospital administrator and said they needed time to clean Ricky up before I could see him. Afterwards, they would send him to the coroner's office to determine cause of death. Once I'd made funeral arrangements, he said, I'd have to call the coroner. Otherwise, the funeral home on rotation would pick up my boy's body.

"How long will he be at the coroner's?" I said.

"I don't know, I'll check," said my pastor.

"You know, on *Quincy*, they're there for days."

He looked at me odd, and said, "Don't try to be superwoman, Sharon."

I didn't know what he meant. My only experience with a coroner was from television, and *Quincy* was the first thing that popped into my mind. What do you think comes to mind when you're in shock? It's not something that will always make sense. I was not being superwoman. I wasn't trying to do everything and control everything. I was like everybody else— wounded, confused, indecisive, doing the best I could.

After a few minutes, they led me to a room in the back. A white sheet wrapped Ricky's body, and I was reminded how small he was. Above the sheet one hand rested over the other. I looked at his face. His eyes always sparkled, and now they were dull. He always had a grin on his face. Now his lips were slightly parted, his mouth a straight line, his skin the color of ash. I bent over him, and touched his hand. It didn't feel cold. It didn't feel real.

"Sharon, this isn't Ricky," said our pastor. "This is the house he lived in."

"I know," I said. "I still want to hold him."

I thought that when I went back to see Ricky, I was going to hold him and tell him that I loved him. I didn't know what a dead child looked like. I couldn't imagine a child so full of life having no life. I thought I would tell Ricky that I would see him soon and to not be afraid and I would never forget him. I wanted to tell him how much joy he had brought us and how proud I was of him.

But I didn't say anything. I didn't pick him up and hold him. I was frozen in disbelief and wonder and felt a sick hollow void seeing my child dead. Ricky wasn't there anymore. He couldn't be. His spirit was in a place I could not reach.

We left the hospital, and when I got to our house, everybody was there, our friends, everyone from church, everybody but Doug. My father called when they were changing planes in Denver and said "The Lord told me that He's going to get us through this." I prayed he was right.

Misty came to me for reassurance. She had a fever, and I was still sick with pneumonia. I put her in the car and we went to the doctor. He gave us shots, and cough syrup for Misty, and sleeping pills for whoever wanted them.

I needed Doug.

Apparently, Doug had gone to a friend's house for a brief visit, and as he backed out of their driveway, they switched on the news and heard about Ricky. They shouted Doug's name, but he was gone. I was at the doctor's office when Doug got home and found vehicles filling the driveway, spilling into the street, and lots of people milling around. He told me days later he thought, Oh, great, Sharon's having a party and didn't tell me.

Terrie took him aside and tried to tell him what happened. Doug was in a jovial mood and horsing around, and wouldn't let her say what she had to. Finally, she yelled at him, "There's been an accident."

He pushed her back. "Don't be stupid," he said.

She was crying and people standing in the driveway and on the front lawn were too. Doug's dad stepped through the crowd, and then our pastor, and Doug knew it was not a party.

"Not Ricky!" he screamed. He could tell from the mournful expressions on people's faces that it was. He charged into the house and slammed open the door to Ricky's empty room, looking for his son.

Then Doug's dad and Pastor Steele accompanied him to the morgue at the hospital. When the attendant showed him the gurney on which Ricky was strapped down, Doug noticed that our child's tooth was broken, and shook him.

"Ricky, wake up," he said.

He shoved Rickey's cart across the room, and ran out. He bolted from the hospital, scaled a six-foot fence, and raced through a field. He told me later that he ran and ran until he dropped to the ground sobbing, beating the ground with his fists.

He blamed himself for Ricky's death—because he saw Ricky seconds before he died. Doug was on his way to install turf on a porch and was traveling northbound on 40th Street, which is a busy two-lane street. He saw Terrie and the kids and pulled over to talk. Ricky leaned in the passenger's window.

"Hey, Spud," said Doug.

"Where ya goin?" said Ricky. "Can I go with you?"

"Sure, but where's Justin?"

"Home," said Ricky.

"You should probably go home because Justin would be mad if he didn't get to go in the truck with us," said Doug.

"Okay," said Ricky, and then he ran with shoelaces undone and flapping on the ground to catch up with Terrie.

Doug pulled away, and Ricky told Terrie he couldn't wait to get home and show me his papers because he had 100s on all of them. When Doug turned the corner at Indian School Road, a car mounted the curb and hit Ricky. Terrie yelled for Doug, but he didn't hear her. So Doug blamed himself. If he had opened the door and taken Ricky with him... But Doug could not see into the future, he was not a psychic, he was not God.

When Doug returned home from the hospital, we didn't talk to each other. If we tried to say something, we cried. We could talk to other people, but not to each other.

My parents arrived that night, and everyone else over the next couple of days. It was good for the kids to have family members around. Still, no one could console my sister Terrie. Dad gave her sleeping pills to quiet her down, she was crying that much. Mom told her she would upset us, and wouldn't let her speak to us. I don't know what was going through people's minds. I didn't blame Terrie for Ricky's death and neither did Doug.

A couple of years younger than me, Terrie had a rough time growing up. She was rebellious, not popular in school, and I was mean to her when we were children. After Terrie started high school, she bloomed, and put my sister Gaile and me to shame. She developed a Barbie-Doll figure, gorgeous legs, and pretty blonde hair. Revenge is sweet, they say. She has deep brown eyes and is a good singer and can harmonize with anyone. Of everyone in our family, she is probably the most humble, the most giving and most loving—and that's saying a lot. If you need help, Terrie would give you the shirt off her back, clean your toilets, and drive you across the world. For someone like Terrie to witness Ricky die in front of her can only have wounded her profoundly, and I pray she has found peace.

That night, Justin went home with his grandma and grandpa to Tempe. Terrie stayed at our place. Doug and I went to bed and tried to sleep, but we couldn't. Doug held me, and we lay there and cried and retched from grief. We cried so much we shook the bed.

The next day, we got up and went to the bank to borrow money to pay for the funeral, and then we staggered through the funeral arrangements. We went to the funeral home, and my dad took charge and said, "Let me handle this. If we don't spend a lot of money, they'll try to make us feel bad."

The funeral director took us to a room filled with big caskets. He said they don't ordinarily stock children's caskets, but they would ship one in from California right away, and we should choose the type and style from the adult caskets. He didn't show us anything gaudy or fancy. He showed us a simple pine box.

Gifts My Father Gave Me

We left the funeral home and drove to the cemetery. The grass was green and the flowers well tended. They gave us a choice of a vault for $400, or a grave liner for $150. We said the liner was fine. I'd expected the worst, but the funeral people were surprisingly bighearted, and didn't charge for services like the cars and chapel.

Next, my sister Gaile took us to the flower shop. We needed a spray of flowers for the casket, and flowers at each end. The ones we liked were $150. All that remained from our loan was $50, and I burst into tears.

"What are the flowers for?" the man said.

"My little boy was run over yesterday," I said.

"On 40th Street?"

"Yes."

"Pick out whatever you want," he said, "and we'll get them there."

I gave him the $50, and he gave us all the flowers we wanted.

Every place we went people tried to make it easy on us. The church members rallied around us. Strangers dropped off food, sodas and water (nobody touched the food until after the funeral). People we'd never met bought money orders at the Circle K and sent them to us. In a few days, we had received over $3,000, more money than we'd seen at one time. The people who rented us our house said we didn't have to pay rent for three months. I was astonished at how supportive, generous and kind everyone was.

The day after Ricky died, my sister Gaile and I and my mom took Justin and his friends to McDonalds for a party. Although Ricky's death would forever darken his birthday celebrations, we wanted Justin to have a semblance of normalcy and to know that in the midst of our sorrow we had not forgotten him. And it seemed many other people felt the same way. Almost all the children in the church up to the sixth grade came and wore funny hats and laughed and played. Children that Justin didn't know but knew about Ricky came to the party and brought presents, not only for Justin, but for Misty, too. Although intensely sad, I was pleased to watch him enjoy himself and feel special.

The next afternoon, my birthday, my dad and brother Bill took Misty, Justin and Bill's boys, Levi, who was four, and Blaine, six, down to the funeral home. On the way in the car, my dad told them they were going to see the *tent* Ricky had lived in. He used the word "tent" because he wanted to frame the discussion in a way they would understand.

We decided to do this instead of having them attend the funeral where they would be exposed to people crying and at times losing control. We felt they were too young to handle it, and at the funeral they would become confused and not get the attention they needed because their parents would be grieving.

Our decision may not be right for everyone's kids. Sometimes it is difficult to know what to do, whether children should or should not attend the funeral. We have to rely on what we know about our children and what we think they can understand and cope with. Every child is different. Each parent has to make this decision, knowing it might not be the best decision. We felt it was more important that our kids saw Ricky somewhere other than at the funeral, and had their own time to talk about what happens when someone dies, and were able to say goodbye in a quiet setting.

After they arrived at the funeral home, my dad and Bill led them to the casket and raised the upper lid. My dad explained that they probably thought they were looking at Ricky, but he was not there. Ricky had moved to a new tent in heaven and was now living with Jesus.

Misty was happy Ricky was wearing the black suit, red bow tie and red cumber bun he'd worn to his aunt's wedding six weeks before. She liked the little red Gideon's Bible he held in his hands. Levi was worried about Ricky's legs. He couldn't see them, and thought if they were broken, Ricky wouldn't be able to walk around in heaven. My dad told him Ricky wouldn't need legs in heaven, but to alleviate his fears he lifted the lid on the rest of the coffin so the children could see that Ricky's legs were all right. He told them that if they felt like crying because they missed Ricky that was okay, and they would get to see him again someday.

The next day at the funeral people said tender, loving things about Ricky. About how well behaved he was, about his infectious grin, about the twinkle in his eye. About how well dressed he was, always.

During the eulogy, our pastor said that Ricky appeared sweet and innocent, but there was a part of Ricky maybe even his mom didn't know about. He said once in awhile he heard a knock on the door and Ricky would be there with a pan of homemade rolls. He'd thank him and give him a dollar.

Whenever I baked bread, I'd tell Ricky to take a pan to the preacher's house. When he returned with his dollar, I asked him why he took the money, and he said the preacher made him take it. What his mom didn't know, explained the preacher during the eulogy, was that sometimes Ricky sneaked a pan of frozen rolls from the freezer, took them to the preacher and got his dollar.

Everyone laughed, and for a moment this broke the numbing sadness of the whole thing.

Ricky stuffed the preacher's money in his piggy bank and gave it to the missionaries or bought something for himself like a pack of gum or a candy bar. He was a virtuous kid, but he had a mischievous side to him. Like one Sunday morning when we left the house heading for church. We met the man who rented it to us, and Ricky said, "Watch my brother," and we turned to Justin who was stumbling along with his shoes pointing in the wrong direction. Ricky said, "His shoes are on the wrong feet. I told him to do that. I tricked him."

Ricky thought tricking someone was very funny.

The funeral ended, and we went home to our house full of people but empty of Ricky. We had to live life without him now, and divided our lives into *Before Ricky* and *After Ricky*.

Before Ricky, I used to bake bread and give it to people. If they were ill or had somebody in the hospital, the fresh bread meant a lot to them. It was symbolic of giving and sharing and loving. *After Ricky*, baking bread seemed pointless. He was not there to deliver the pan to the preacher and earn his dollar.

The first year without him there were times I thought, Why weren't all the kids killed at once and then I wouldn't have to live? I wouldn't have to function. I wouldn't have to get out of bed everyday. I wouldn't have to love. I wouldn't have to hurt anymore. I didn't have that way out. Misty and Justin were four- and five-years-old, and they demanded my attention. They didn't lie in bed all day and cry. They didn't want to die.

Doug and I used to say, "Okay, if the Lord came to us and said—"

> *Doug and Sharon, one of you can be with Ricky, and one of you has to stay here. Who will it be?*

—then we would argue about who would go. We did this in front of Misty and Justin, and can you imagine how they felt? We argued about who would leave instead of who would stay with them. That life wasn't worth living for them. Our thinking was messed up with our grief, and the day I understood what I was doing, I stopped.

Gifts My Father Gave Me

I know that wasn't how I truly felt. I wanted to be with Ricky, but I wanted to be with Misty and Justin too. I loved them and could still fix things for them. With Ricky, I couldn't fix anything anymore. I felt helpless. Because I always fixed things. Fixing was something I learned from my dad. Whenever one of my kids was sick or hurt or in trouble, I fixed it. Not this time.

The night after Ricky died my mom and dad and I sat at the kitchen table and dad cried.

"Not only have I lost Ricky," he said, "my daughter lost her son and I can't do anything about it."

"Dad, you've already helped me," I said. "You taught me about the Lord. You taught me to have faith, and to hope. You've given me the tools I need to live."

"I can't fix it for you," he said.

"It's not up to you to fix," I said. "The Lord could have prevented Ricky's death. He could've put His hand down and stopped the car."

He didn't because it's not up to God to fix things. He gave us free will, and sometimes with free will a man will drive a car up on a sidewalk and kill your baby. God allows us freedom to make choices. And sometimes we make bad ones. The man who killed Ricky will live with his choice the rest of his life.

So will I.

It was not my fault, but it became my judgment, and a sentence to a life empty of my child's presence. Life in prison could not have wounded me as much. It was a stab through the heart.

Ricky Dale Knutson, my darling boy, that bright light of happiness, was born on the 29th of April, 1976, and died the 22nd of February, 1983, one day before Justin's fifth birthday, two days before I turned twenty-four.

We buried him the day after my birthday. He was six-years-old... and he always will be.

"Let the little children come to Me..."

—Luke 18:16

"And God shall wipe away all tears from their eyes; and there shall be no more death, neither sorrow, nor crying, neither shall there be any more pain: for the former things are passed away."

—Revelation 21:4

Chapter 14

Once Upon A Time

A couple of weeks after the funeral, Misty asked to see where Ricky went to heaven.

She was afraid, and we moved hesitantly down the street, my four-year-old and I, hand-in-hand, and stepped lightly up to the spot where Ricky was struck. The sidewalk was still splattered with his blood. A tree was gashed where the car had hit it, a piece of bark lay shattered on the ground. I was already sorry for having taken her. If I'd been thinking straight, I probably would not have.

Misty suddenly looked up at me, and I thought she was going to comment on the blood. "Mom, where's Ricky's shoes?"

The impact had knocked Ricky out of his shoes, and they were on the sidewalk when I had arrived at the scene.

"Misty, the policemen figured Ricky wasn't going to need 'em again," I said. "We threw them away." I regretted the words as they spilled out of my mouth.

"Whewww... I'm glad he's not going to get heaven all dirty."

I was too stunned and saddened to laugh. Although today when I think of what she said, I do.

Gifts My Father Gave Me

Kids say things you never forget. When Justin was in second grade, he wrote about Ricky—

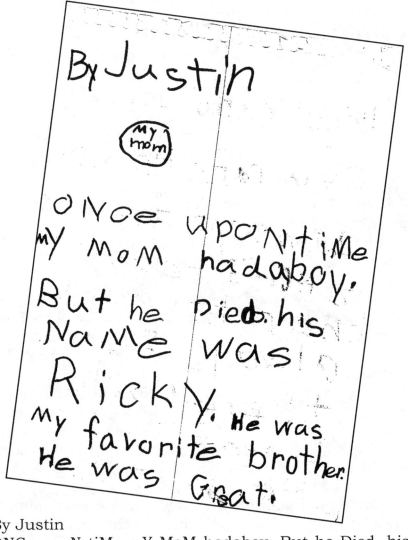

By Justin
ONCe upoN tiMe mY MoM hadaboy. But he Died. his NaMe was Ricky. He was My favorite brother. He was Great.

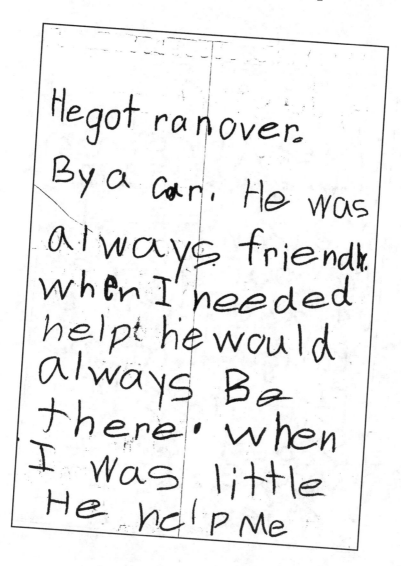

He got ranover. By a car.
He was always friendly. when I needed helpt he would
always Be there. when I was little He help Me

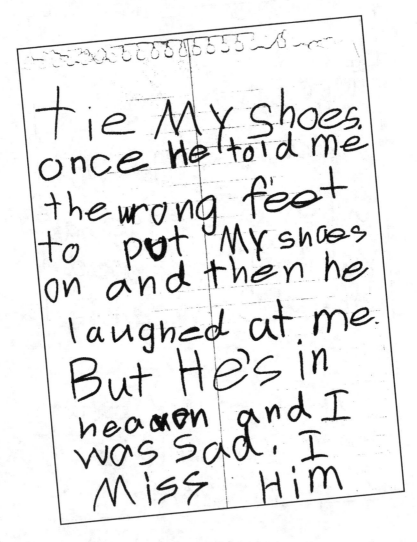

tie My shoes. once He told me the wrong feet to put My shoes on and then he laughed at me. But He's in heavon and I was Sad. I Miss Him

I missed him, too, and didn't know how I'd bear the pain. My sister Gaile didn't know how I would either. She was worried about me, and nine days after Ricky was killed, she phoned me from the hospital delivery room where she had moments before given birth to her firstborn son, Jaye.

"Russ and I talked about it, and you can have Jaye if you want him, but you have to decide before we get attached to him," she said.

This was a gift beyond anything I could have anticipated. A mother willing to give up her newborn. A sister who loved me that much. I had to turn them down, of course. I couldn't accept their baby as a replacement for Ricky, as loving and well-meaning the intent. This would not alleviate my grief, and I had to find my own way of coping with Ricky's loss.

One of the things I did to try to relieve my sadness was to give my two living kids what Ricky never had, and I went on a buying spree. Whatever my kids wanted, they had.

In kindergarten, Ricky loved Capri Sun juice boxes, and often begged me for them. They were expensive, and I'd tell him we couldn't afford them. I made Kool-Aid instead and put it in his thermos, but the other kids had juice boxes, and he longed for them. Once he was going on a field trip and I bought him a Capri Sun and he was elated.

After he was gone, I went down to Costco and bought cases of them because I didn't want Misty and Justin not to have them like their brother.

Before Ricky died, I took the kids to the mall. Misty was in a stroller and Justin and Ricky walked next to me. A shoe salesman stepped outside his store and asked if I'd ever had my children's feet measured. He said I was ruining their feet if I hadn't. I checked the cost of the shoes, and the cheapest was $20. I didn't spend that much on my own shoes. After Ricky died, I was in the mall with Misty and Justin and was about to pass the Stride Rite shoe store, and all of sudden became obsessed with getting my kids' feet measured. I bought them three pairs of good shoes a piece and spent almost $200. I wept because Ricky never got his feet measured.

The first Christmas after Ricky died, I bought them everything I thought they wanted, regardless of cost. And on Christmas night when I went into Justin's room to say goodnight, I asked him if he had had a good Christmas and liked the things we bought him. "I just wanted a brother for Christmas," he said.

My buying binges didn't help our financial situation. We were trying to pay off our medical expenses, and then we were hit with the funeral costs. People helped us out, but we had a lot to cover, and our expenses were mounting.

Doug hardly worked, he didn't have the heart anymore. He spent a great deal of time at the cemetery sitting by Ricky's grave. People would call and say they were interested in new carpet and I'd set up an appointment. I'd tell Doug to take samples over and measure for the carpeting, and sometimes he wouldn't show up. He was apathetic, as if he'd died with Ricky. I reminded him we had two kids to feed and had to go on living.

To help us out with the bills, Doug and I discussed suing the driver of the car that killed Ricky, and we called Doug's uncle, a Texas attorney specializing in wrongful death suits. He said the driver's father was a big-shot attorney and would fight us. We could wait years for a settlement. "It will eat you up and destroy your lives," Doug's uncle said. He recommended that we accept the limit of the car insurance and walk away. Especially since we had urgent financial needs.

We thought this was a good plan, and Doug's uncle sent a letter to the driver's insurance company saying we would not pursue their client beyond what his car insurance covered. We wanted a quick settlement. That's not what we got.

About six months after Ricky was killed, I called the insurance company and asked why I hadn't heard from them. They said the agent is on vacation, the file is not complete, blah, blah, blah, we'll call you in a week. They didn't call in a week. They didn't call in two weeks. I called again and was told the agent would call me back in a few minutes. He didn't. The next day, I called yet again, and the agent came to the phone.

"We don't have all the documents to complete the case," he said.

"What do you need?" I said.

"A statement from Ricky's doctor about his health when he was killed."

"What do you mean?"

"Did he have any diseases."

"What difference does it make if he had a disease?" I said.

"Well, if he had leukemia, and his life expectancy was only three years, we would pay a different amount of money. We wouldn't owe you as much."

"He was well enough to walk down the street," I screamed. "And if he only had one day to live, your client took it from him and took him from us."

"We need proof that..."

"You'll get it," I said, and hung up.

The agent faxed a form to our church office, and I took it to the doctor. The doctor wrote that Ricky was in good health, had no diseases, no illnesses. He was a typical six-year-old boy.

Then I got in the car, sat Misty and Justin next to me, and drove to the insurance company. We entered the insurance company's office, Misty in one hand, Justin in the other, a photo album under my arm, and I asked to see the agent.

"He's in a meeting," said the receptionist.

"I'll wait," I said.

"We don't know how long he'll be."

"That's fine. I'll wait for him," I said, and gently set the photo album on the magazine table.

I sat down, with two kids, four- and five-years-old. They were good, they sat still, they knew this was important. It had to do with their brother, and why he wasn't here anymore.

You often hear about how resilient children are when bad things happen. But sometimes we forget that they grieve as much as adults. Misty had terrible nightmares, and was afraid of cars in parking lots. She thought they were going to run her over. She asked a lot of questions about the man who killed Ricky. "Does he still drive? Does he take drugs? Is he going to jail?" She asked about Ricky. "Will Jesus see Ricky wearing a bloody shirt? Will Jesus fix the hole in Ricky's head?" Justin was the opposite. He was quiet, and held everything in, which is more typical of how children respond to trauma. He mentioned Ricky's death only occasionally.

At the insurance company, people arrived and filled the seats in the waiting room, and one by one drifted down the hallway to their appointments and later strolled out and left, and new people arrived and waited. Then I saw the agent in the hallway. He glanced my way, and then turned his back to me. I picked up the photo album, told my children to follow me, and called his name.

"Excuse me, do you have an appointment?" he said.

"Yes, I do," I lied. "Maybe you don't remember me. I'm Sharon Knutson, Ricky's mom. Your client ran over my son."

"Okay."

"You need a statement about Ricky's health. I have it, and I want you to pull his file and guarantee me that when I leave here, there is nothing else you need."

"This isn't necessary Mrs. *Ka-newt-son...*" he said.

"It's not? Then why is it six months after Ricky's death and you're telling me I need more documents. We settled three months ago, we signed your papers, and there is still no check. Why? Because you are concerned about my dead son's state of health?"

"This is just a procedure, Mrs. *Ka-newt-son,*" he said.

"It's an unnecessary procedure. And my question to you is, if he is worth less if he had a disease, is he worth more if he was an exceptionally good-looking kid?"

"Really, Mrs. *Ka-newt-son...*"

"The name is Knutson. *Nut-son.* The *K* is silent. And my son's name is Ricky Knutson. And these are my other children, Misty and Justin. *Mis-ty. Jus-tin.*"

"This is not necessary," he reiterated.

"You're right. It was not necessary for me to come here." I pulled the doctor's letter from the album. "It was not necessary for you to have this form letter."

My voice was growing louder.

"Why don't we go back to my office."

"No!" I said. "I want everyone in the waiting room to hear how cold-hearted you are and what a criminal outfit you're running."

He was silent.

"Do you have kids or grandkids?" I said.

"I have a grandson."

"How much is he worth?"

His face didn't change expression. It was sour and indifferent.

"Tell me how much he is worth."

Everyone in the waiting room was watching, frozen in mid action, holding up a newspaper, leaning in to talk to a friend, suspending a cup of coffee to the lips. Eyes astounded.

"Why don't you ask my kids how much they want to sell their brother for?" I said. "How much money will make them feel better about their brother being run over?

Then I took my children's hands, led them into his office and sat down. He followed, and I laid the album on the table and opened it to a picture of Ricky. The agent dutifully looked, and an exceptionally handsome boy stared out at him. I turned to another photo and then another and another and tears trickled down my face.

"We could have sued your client for millions of dollars, but we didn't," I said. "We don't have years to wait for a trial. We need the money now to pay for his funeral, and I have to care for my other children. We have bills we can't pay. We treated you with respect, and all you've done is treat us like trash. You've acted as if my son's life is worth nothing."

He didn't reply, and for the next half hour sat there and listened. When I was done, he said he would process the check right away and mail it to us.

"Oh, no, you're not," I said. "You call me the moment it's printed and I will be here to pick it up."

We left, and I shook for days afterwards. I was not used to confronting people like this. I was taught to be respectful and polite, but this was about my son. Who I would never wrap my arms around and hug again.

Late on a Friday ten days after the confrontation, the agent phoned me and said the check was ready. I went down and picked it up. I had to wait until Monday to deposit it, and Doug and I went first thing to the bank with the intention of paying off our truck loan, and the medical bills, and then going shopping for groceries. All weekend I thought about how helpful the money was going to be. It would not bring my son back, but it would give us a little support and help my other children.

We stood in line and I handed the teller the check and told her to deposit it, and give us some cash, I had to go to the store.

"I'm sorry," she said, "we have to put a ten-day hold on it."

"Why?" I said.

"This isn't a check," she said. "It's a bank draft."

"I have to buy food."

She brought the manager over who said the funds were not guaranteed and I'd have to wait ten days. I had $100,000 in my hand but I couldn't buy a carton of milk. This was another kick when Doug and I were at our lowest emotionally. We were hurting and yet the insurance company took advantage of that to delay the payment we needed desperately.

I called the insurance company right there from the bank. "Why did you give me a check that's not guaranteed?" I demanded to know. We argued back and forth, and eventually they instructed the bank to release a third of the money.

I was finally finished with the insurance company and their callous hearts, yet in spite of the misery they caused us, there was some good that ultimately came from the experience. When I met people after that who had suffered catastrophic losses in their lives, I gave them a gift—knowledge. Hard-earned knowledge.

I told them: Be prepared to fight, never give an inch, never give up, because the insurance companies will do everything they can to stall and demean your loss. I told people about using direct deposit to avoid a bank draft with a hold on its funds. I guided them over the trip wires so they wouldn't become bitter and consumed. I told them what to expect from funeral homes, from the coroner, from the justice system. I understand what people are going through. Not only are they struggling to cope with their unspeakable loss, but they are forced to combat the idiots of the world who take advantage of their confusion and grief.

To put things in perspective, the heartache caused by the insurance company was a pin prick compared to the anguish of losing our child. That pain was staggering, and relentless, and each day that followed Ricky's death felt insurmountable. Things did not seem to get better with time. Each day made us more unbelieving that such a thing could happen to him, to us, to our family. To lose someone you love is the hardest thing in the world.

I knew when we put Ricky's body in the grave, it wasn't the end of his life. It was the end as we conceive of it here on earth. Ricky was now in his spirit body, with God, in a far better place. I also knew it was going to be a long time before I saw him again, and I couldn't comprehend how long that separation would be.

I turned to God like never before and eventually that's what got me through the sorrow. My faith in believing Ricky was with Jesus gave me hope. It was faith that helped me understand the blessing Ricky had given me two nights before he died. He had reminded me of the time he thought Jesus had visited him. Ricky died believing Jesus loved him. I reminded Doug of this, but he was too preoccupied with his own grief to think about anything else. Doug said it was *his* fault that Ricky died. God was punishing him for what he'd done to me.

I told my dad what he had said. "If this is how God punishes us for what we do, we'd all be dead," he told Doug. "God doesn't work that way. Ricky died because somebody drove up on a sidewalk and ran over him. It's not because you were unfaithful to Sharon."

He listened to what my dad said, but didn't get it. He understood it intellectually. He didn't grasp it emotionally or spiritually. He felt guilty, and it took him a long time to accept he was not at fault.

Months went by and our grief was bottomless. Almost a year had passed, and still we suffered from our loss. We pined and brooded and wept. But now we had to face a great challenge, and I didn't know how we would do it. We were obliged to display our sorrow in a public venue, the courts.

The man who killed our child was going on trial.

Chapter 15

The Trial

C ole Sorenson was not charged for running over my son. He was not charged for driving up on the sidewalk. He was not charged for driving while impaired, nor for exceeding the speed limit. Not even for destruction of private property (damaging the tree). He was charged with nothing.

I called the police station. I called it everyday. I was told the detective was out of the office on a case, he was on the phone, he was on vacation, the lab work hadn't come back yet. It was always something. Why was the process slow and difficult? There were witnesses, tire marks, blood work.

By accident, I found out what the problem was. I wish I could say it was incompetence or drunkenness or a monumental workload that prevented the police and the justice system from grinding its wheels forward.

Doug was laying carpet for Jim Meredith, our representative in the Arizona House of Representatives, and Jim asked what happened to the man who killed our son. Doug filled him in on my struggle with the police department. Outraged, Jim called the county attorney for an update, and here's the gist of the county attorney's response:

Gifts My Father Gave Me

> Cole Sorenson's dad is a prominent attorney. His grandfather is a prominent attorney. You know they're going to get him off. We don't want to waste state money prosecuting him. The Knutsons? These people are nobody.

Jim Meredith said the Knutsons were his constituents, and he demanded that the county attorney do something.

The county attorney presented the case to seven deputy county attorneys and asked for their recommendations. Five voted *No* to prosecute, and two voted *Yes*. Lynn Hamilton, who had a boy Ricky's age, said she'd like to handle the case. The county attorney said fine, but she was not to spend money on expert witnesses. And she was to do it on her own time.

Here we had a deputy county attorney prosecuting the case whenever she could fit us in, and she wasn't allowed to pay for expert help. Cole Sorenson's family, on the other hand, hired two of the highest paid criminal defense attorneys in Arizona. And they had what seemed like unlimited resources for calling expert witnesses to the stand.

All we wanted was the man who killed Ricky to pay for his crime and be charged with vehicular manslaughter. Lynn told us that would never happen, and the best we could do was a plea bargain.

"I want him to go to trial," I told her. "I want his recklessness exposed to the world."

"You don't understand," she said. "Trust me."

The deal was for him to plead *no contest*, which meant he would accept the punishment without acknowledging guilt. This allowed him to offer the judge mitigating circumstances in his defense. It also meant that after the criminal procedure was over, we could not use the *no contest* plea against him if we decided to sue him civilly. A clever ploy.

I felt like I was negotiating not for the meaning of my son's life, but for the inconvenience of his death. What was his death worth in the justice system? How much accountability for killing a *nobody*? I felt like I was on the Titanic where the steerage passengers were forced to wait below deck while the ship was sinking to let the rich off first. As we all know, few of the poor managed to get past the steel gates and slip into a lifeboat.

In the plea arrangement, Cole agreed to "one count of endangerment and one count of solicitation to possess a narcotic drug." But the county attorney did get something more. Cole's attorneys agreed to Class 6 "open-end offenses," which let the judge decide if the charges should be misdemeanors or felonies.

Before long, we received a phone call from the other side's high-priced attorneys. They invited us to their plush office for a deposition. We were to reveal what we intended to do, and they would tell us what they were going to do. Doug and I sat down on a leather couch. Cole was not present. One of his attorneys stood over us and started up like a windup doll, and the exchange went something like this:

"This poor young man..." said the attorney.

For a moment, I thought he was talking about Ricky. I should have known better.

"This poor young man," he went on, "is in the prime of his life. He had a seizure and accidentally ran over your son, and you want him to go to prison where he'll become someone's little sweetheart."

What seizure? I wondered.

"I understand you are Christians, whatever that is."

"Yes, I am a Christian," I said.

"I go to church every Easter with my wife," he said. "That's the extent of my beliefs."

"Okay," I said.

"I want you to know where I'm coming from."

"Okay."

"Tell me, is it a Christian belief to punish this boy for having a seizure and an accident? Is it Christian to force him into prison and ruin his life?"

"First of all, you are putting words in my mouth," I said. "And why do you think he had a seizure?"

He plopped down several doctors' reports on a shiny coffee table.

"Show me," I said.

He flipped open a report and pointed to a page that said Cole had had a seizure when he was a child.

"A person at the scene said it looked like he was yawning," the lawyer said. "And according to the doctor, he bit his tongue, and had abnormal brain waves, which are prevalent in people that have seizures."

"He bit his tongue because he ran into a tree," I said "This doesn't prove anything. Is he on medication?"

"Well... his parents don't want him labeled an epileptic."

"You're saying he has fits and he's allowed to drive?"

"He has to get to his job."

"If your son has epileptic seizures and you don't want him on medication because he might be labeled, would you give him your car? I don't think so."

The attorney was silent.

"This man is twenty-years-old," I said. "He's in good shape, not one who has seizures. And if he goes to jail and becomes someone's sweetheart, that's a prison problem, not my problem."

The deposition was soon over, but it was a chilling rehearsal for the main event—the sentencing hearing in front of a judge. The hearing date was set for October.

It was postponed.

Not knowing if I'd get to say what I wanted to in court, Doug and I wrote the judge a letter. Here's part of it:

10/29/1983

Dear (Judge Howe):

...our feelings and thoughts are based on our relationship with the Lord. We have expressed to Cole himself that we do not hate him or want to destroy his life or his family. We do not seek personal revenge for there is absolutely nothing that can bring our son back to life or replace him.

We have had many nights of sleep disrupted by piercing screams as our daughter awoke from a nightmare of a car running over Ricky and seeing him flying through the air and... land with a big hole in his head.

Our son (Justin's) much anticipated birthday party was... darkened by the untimely death of his brother (who) was his hero.

My birthday, the 24th (of February), will never be completely happy again as my mind will always think of... preparing for Ricky's funeral...

We hope that you will be wise and see that the law must be enforced and that wealth or influence can not permit... a slap on the hands.

Sincerely,
Doug & Sharon Knutson

Gifts My Father Gave Me

Then the hearing was set for November. It was postponed again. Then December. Postponed.

My parents flew out each time to be with us. My dad took time off work.

January. Postponed.

Finally, the hearing in Superior Court in Phoenix was called for February, one year after Ricky was killed. There were three days of hearings, and Cole's family hired an expert witness who sat on the stand and said that Cole had had an epileptic seizure.

Cocaine? Cole claimed he hadn't taken any, even though a vial of cocaine was found in his car. The authorities waited six weeks before they tested his blood sample, but that wasn't the real issue. They didn't perform the correct drug test for cocaine and they could not retest his blood since they had failed to preserve it.

After the defense attorney got me on the stand, he tried again to embarrass and intimidate me. He never called me by my correct name. *Newt-son.* What is it with my name? The insurance man tried to belittle me with the same tactic. And the attorney referred to Ricky as a little girl. He described the accident scene over and over again, either to upset me or to convince the judge that it *was* an accident.

You would think he would be kind and considerate to the grieving mother, but he wasn't. He quoted Scripture, which was a laugh coming from an Easter Sunday church goer who, during the deposition, professed to know nothing about Christianity, and was arrogant enough to brag about his ignorance.

The following is an excerpt from the court transcripts.

"...you're recommending that the Court sentence Mr. Sorenson to the maximum possible crime, maximum possible penalty, are you not?" said the lawyer.

"That's true," I said.

"And I believe you've told us that that's based on your Christian doctrine, is it not?"

"Not completely based on it, but I'm sure that's a contributing factor."

"When you say you and your husband talked over this Christian doctrine and consulted your Bible teachings to come up with this recommendation, did you overlook those doctrines of 'Vengeance is mine, saith the Lord?' Did you overlook Christian forgiveness?"

"No sir, we did not."

"You took those into consideration?"

"Yes, sir. You know, it's... hard for me to discuss Christianity with you when you have no part of it. It's like you speak in French and me speaking Spanish. We can't communicate."

The defense attorney interrogated me as if I were the one on trial for killing a child, and as I sat on the stand waiting for the next disrespectful question, I thought about the night before the hearing. My brother Ande had called and said, "Remember, you have nothing to lose tomorrow. They can't take anything from you. Ricky's not going to die again."

After the phone call, I prayed and asked God for help. I wanted Cole held accountable. But there was part of me that thought, I don't know what happened that day. I wasn't there. I thought about his mom, how distressing it must be for her to sit in court, thinking her son might go to prison.

After she took the stand, she talked about her son's amphetamine use. She had given him diet pills, which contained amphetamine, to keep him awake to study for exams. She didn't see anything wrong with it, all the students were doing it. I shouldn't be too harsh on her. Mothers have a tough time figuring out their kids and the times they live in.

My sympathy for Cole's mother, however, didn't stop me from giving back to the defense attorney as good as I got. This was my son he was talking about. Certainly Ricky was not going to die again, but I would not let anybody poison his memory, which would have had the effect of killing him again. At forever six-years-old, Ricky could not defend himself, not when he was alive, he was too young, and not when he was dead. But *I* could defend him. I was his voice and his mother. I am his mother still.

The defense attorney didn't act like my being Ricky's mother signified anything. But in that courtroom, I did my best to impress upon him that he had his job, and I had mine. His job was to tear down, to desecrate, to vandalize the life and death of a baby. My job was to praise and honor Ricky, and with sharp teeth, stand my ground.

The hearing continued with rancor and insults pouring from him like spoiled soup. I thought, Do your worst, because I have nothing to lose, and no matter how much he tried to provoke me, I held my own and did not cry or lose my temper.

In the end, the judge charged Cole Sorenson with two felonies and sentenced him to eighteen months in prison. Apparently, the judge based his decision on the tragic consequences of the accident and Cole's admission that he was subject to seizures, whether real or not, yet continued to drive a car.

In the courtroom were my mother, in-laws, pastor and many church friends. My father couldn't make it this time. Upon hearing the judge's ruling, people erupted with clapping. I felt someone pat me on the back. Somebody said I put that lawyer in his place. I don't think I did anything, and I didn't feel like clapping, or smiling, or saying anything.

I hung my head down and sobbed. It was as if I were sitting there watching myself. I was shedding tears, but at peace. I'd prayed to the Lord to give me the right words, and they were there when I needed them. I felt horrible for Cole's mom because the authorities were going to take him away, and who knew what might happen behind bars.

Nobody won that day. Cole didn't, his family didn't, the lawyers didn't, and Doug and our family didn't. Justice was served, that was all, and as we stepped out of the courtroom to the outside, I felt a cool wind whisper across the desert. The breeze felt like Ricky saying, "You did good, mom. You tricked them."

That night, the court reporter phoned me. "I've never seen anybody in court behave like you," she said. "You were peaceful and sensible and it doesn't appear that you have an ounce of bitterness. I don't understand this Christianity thing, but whatever it is must be *amazing*."

She chose the right word.

Chapter 16

The Truth

*V*ictory, if that's what it was, was bittersweet. Cole's sentence was reduced, and he served fourteen months.

After he got out of prison, I had a feeling something wasn't right, and asked a friend of mine, a private detective, to check into Cole's release. She soon called with bad news. Cole's record had been expunged, erased, as if the whole incident never happened.

Did that mean Ricky's death would be expunged, too? Could Ricky now go on with his life, too? Would I get to see my son grow up, graduate from school, get a job, get married, have children, too?

Bad news? I don't know. Is it bad that Cole could go on with his life? That despite what he had done, life offered him a chance at happiness? I think it was divine intervention that allowed him to start again, but he was living a lie. He never told the truth about what happened, and that was a greater prison than the one he'd been incarcerated in. The lie was prison without end. When he closed his eyes at bedtime, he could not rest. The lie would never sleep.

Before long, Cole attended law school and then applied to the Arizona State Bar to take the bar exam and acquire his license to practice. Lawyering ran in his family. His

Gifts My Father Gave Me

father was a lawyer, his grandfather was one, and now it was his turn.

I wrote a letter to the State Bar Committee. In doing a full background investigation of their lawyers-to-be, they called and asked me to attend a hearing. They weren't interested in what I might settle for. They didn't care who was represented by the most expensive attorney. They didn't consider whether I was a somebody or a nobody. They wanted information to help them decide if Cole Sorenson should serve the people of the State of Arizona.

They wanted the truth. I intended to give them an earful.

On the day of the hearing, we shuffled into an enormous conference room and settled along a large table. Cole entered with his father. Doug and my dad sat on either side of me. About five or six people from the State Bar sat down. They requested our comments first, and then they would let Cole respond.

I began...

"It bothers me that he seems to have no remorse," I said. "Cole killed my son. He received punishment, and served some time, and then his record was erased, as if my son's death never happened. Now he wants to be an attorney. His life is going on. My son didn't get to play Little League ball."

Tears trickled from Cole's eyes and down his face.

"When we were in the courtroom, and I got up to take the stand, Cole left the room. He didn't have to sit there and listen to me tell about my son. I think that's wrong. He should hear everything about Ricky. He should hear about our loss and grief. But he didn't have the balls to sit in the courtroom and listen to what he did."

Then I described Cole's irresponsible lifestyle. How he was suspected of stealing from a convenience store, was arrested twice for drug possession, had two speeding convictions and two serious car accidents resulting in injury, including my son's death. He had admitted to occasionally overindulging in alcohol, and using illegal drugs such as marijuana, cocaine and speed.

Who ultimately paid for his self-indulgence? Who paid for his fun? My son, my family. But it wasn't all Cole's fault. Cole's father bought him out of everything he'd ever done bad in his life. He bought him the Camaro muscle car that drove up on the sidewalk, slammed into Ricky, and hurled him thirty feet in the air. He bought Cole the car that didn't brake or stop until it smashed into a tree.

"Because Cole's father would not make his son pay the consequences for his wrong deeds," I said, "my son is dead. And now all Cole's family cares about is that he gets to practice law."

Cole brushed the back of his hands across his eyes, but the tears would not stop.

"I have a hard time believing he had an epileptic seizure. He didn't take medication. He never quit driving. Why would you drive if you had epilepsy? We know he didn't get up that morning and decide to kill somebody. But he is responsible. I know what happened that day, and you, Cole, know what happened, and it wasn't a seizure. It was the result of an out-of-control lifestyle. Now what? Will daddy buy you out of this one and into the State Bar?"

I was finished with what I had to say. Everyone was quiet, studying their reflections in the glossy table top. I could hear the air whirring through the vents. Then Cole spoke. At last.

"They told me not to say anything," he said. "They said they were going to do the talking, and say I had a seizure. I never had a seizure, but I didn't know I could tell the truth. My dad handled everything, and I was told to keep my mouth shut. I wanted to tell you I was sorry, but they said you wanted me to go to jail for the rest of my life."

He continued, "I didn't snort cocaine that day, but I had snorted cocaine over the weekend. I took diet pills to stay up and study, and I fell asleep at the wheel and ran over your son. I'm responsible for killing your son. I'm sorry. I'm sorry..."

Another moment of silence passed. The cool air was suddenly biting and hot, and I was lightheaded. I felt something drain out of me. It was rage, and bitterness, hopelessness and despair.

"We wanted the truth," I said. "That's all we ever wanted, and the truth sets you free."

A man from the Bar turned to me and said, "What is your recommendation?"

"Do whatever you feel is right," I said. "We forgive him."

Then I looked at his father and said, "I talked to our pastor and he asked me if I could forgive you for doing what you thought was good for your son, as a father who loves his child. You showed bad judgment, and my family has paid for it. I don't forgive you, but I'm working on it."

His father said nothing.

Look at Cole's life. His father didn't give him any gifts. By bailing him out repeatedly, he didn't let his son learn life's lessons, and look what it has cost him, look at what he's lost. His dad never allowed him to lose anything and he lost nearly everything.

Our forgiveness helped the State Bar officials make a decision about Cole. They would admit him to the Bar. He became an attorney, and achieved his dream. Cole's wife phoned me one day and said that after we forgave Cole, "You gave him his life back. Your forgiveness set him free."

Maybe our forgiveness set him free from his obligation to us, but I don't think he forgave himself. I found
out soon after the State Bar meeting that Cole had had
the numbers—

2-22-83

—tattooed on his ankle, which
was the day Ricky was killed. He wanted to be reminded
every morning when he got up and put on his socks
that he was responsible. Cole used it as a reminder that
he had to make a difference for two people's lives that
day—his life and Ricky's.

After the hearing, I received a note from Cole's mother.

> For years I have agonized over you... (My
> husband) tells me that you testified you are
> a close and happy family. To me, that was the
> most important statement made that day.
>
> Cole has always been the nicest per-
> son, from a little boy, to manhood. To know
> that he caused the death of a darling little
> boy, and hideous unhappiness to a lovely
> family, was a heavy load you have helped
> to lighten a little.
>
> In my prayers, almost every night, I
> have asked Heavenly Father to help your
> children to always be a delight to you and
> to help you have a wonderful life together.
>
> Sincerely,
> Carolyn Sorenson

A short time later, I invited Cole and his wife to attend
church with us and to come over for lunch afterwards.

Gifts My Father Gave Me

The get-together went fine, and didn't have the undercurrent I feared it might. When they were ready to leave, Cole told Misty and Justin that if there was ever anything he could do to help, they should call on him, and he said how sorry he was for taking their brother's life.

"Oh, that's okay," said Misty who was in first grade. "It's better for us to lose a brother than for us to have killed somebody. It has to be worse for you."

Chapter 17

Healing

O ver the years people have asked how I'm doing. Have I gotten over Ricky's death, is it easier with each passing day? I wondered for a long time when I would get over Ricky's loss, and one day realized I would never get over it.

Every morning when I woke up my first thought was, Ricky's not here, and I was going to face the day without him. It didn't mean I'd go back to bed and hide. It didn't mean I couldn't make breakfast and talk to my family and go to the mall. It was that his absence was so present. The space he'd inhabited was there, like a shell waiting to be filled.

Then I got up one morning about seven years after he had died, and I realized that I didn't think about Ricky yesterday. Oh, my gosh, I forgot my child. How could I forget my child? Then I thought, What a relief. I can go through a day without thinking that Ricky isn't here. Because that's negative. That was my first thought, and it set the tone for the rest of the day, and made me depressed. Not thinking about Ricky for even one day was a sign that I was healing.

And there was a sign that Doug was healing, too. The day Ricky was killed, I was sick in bed, and Doug made pancakes for breakfast, Ricky's favorite. After that, Doug couldn't bring himself to make them anymore. I think they reminded him of Ricky's death. Then a year later I saw him in the kitchen making pancakes for Misty and Justin.

"Hey, you're fixing pancakes," I said, and he looked at me like I was crazy. I said, "You haven't fixed pancakes since Ricky died."

He had a surprised look in his eyes. He hadn't realized. It made him sad instantly, because remembering enslaved him. It held onto him and he could not escape. However, once he broke the chain, once he forgot for a moment that Ricky was dead, remembering no longer had power over him, and the next time he fixed pancakes, thinking about Ricky was a little easier. It didn't mean he forgot Ricky. It didn't mean he forgot the pain. It meant he was able to get up in the morning, feel better about himself, and get on with the day God gave him to enjoy.

It was a similar situation with Christmas. For the longest time, I couldn't decorate the house or the tree because it was too painful to take out the homemade Christmas ornaments that Ricky had made in school or the ones my mom bought for each grandkid every year with their names engraved on them. I couldn't bring myself to hang up only two stockings and leave Ricky's in the box.

Misty was the one who took it upon herself to try to bring us cheer. She decorated the house for several years until one Christmas I realized I was cheating Misty and Justin out of a very special holiday. So I started decorating again, and the act itself helped me in the grieving and healing process. I discovered that sometimes I had to do things that hurt even when I didn't want to because in the long run they helped.

Healing

It's now over twenty years since Ricky died, and I don't remember him much anymore. I don't remember what it was like to have him around me everyday. There were years when I didn't think about Ricky for weeks at a time. Sometimes something would trigger a thought about Ricky, but I can't create new memories of him. I only have the same memories, and what I ended up doing was dividing my life into sections like in a filing cabinet, and when no new information came about Ricky, I slid in a divider.

The more files or memories I accumulated *after* Ricky's death, the more space they took up, and the files of him from *before* his death became a smaller and smaller part of my life. After that, thinking about Ricky's death, and even his life, was not as overwhelming as it had been. Every file was there. Every memory was there, it was still him, but I was not as crushed by the memory. I hadn't gotten over his death, but things got better. Life got better. Living got better.

We had a strong support group and great friends. A lot of those friends stayed friends, and whenever I saw the old friends, my memories of them with Ricky returned and I dived back into those files. But after awhile, I made new memories with the old friends and stuck new files into the *after* Ricky section, and they are memories without Ricky.

Some people who have incurred a tragic loss resent their old friends because they remind them of their loss, and sometimes they dump them. They don't want to be reminded that their friends' children lived, and *my child didn't*. I was not like that. I didn't look at someone's son and think, Why couldn't he have died instead of Ricky? I cherish their children, and I'm glad they are alive and happy. I love my old friends. They were there when I needed them, and when they need me, I'm here for them.

Gifts My Father Gave Me

Besides spending time with our old friends, we went on to make new friends, and they had no memory of Ricky or our loss. For instance, about ten years after Ricky's death, I walked into our new pastor's office, sat down, and said earnestly, "You can never know me." Poor guy. What was I doing to him? You can envision him sitting behind his big desk and not understanding what the heck I was talking about.

I told him we were glad that he and his wife and children had come to the church, and we were looking forward to becoming friends and working together, but there was part of me he'd never know. "Because you think of me as Misty and Justin's mom," I said, "and I'm Misty and Justin and Ricky's mom. But you'll never know Ricky and that part of me."

He looked at me like, so? How was he supposed to respond? I've been told that some people give their new friends a hard time about their loss. I'm no exception, and I was being unfair to the pastor.

The healing process took a long time. I can't say how many years because it was gradual and I hardly noticed it was taking place. For me, healing had a lot to do with forgiveness—forgiving the man who ran over Ricky, and forgiving myself for feeling guilty about forgiving him. I believe I forgave Cole even before the court hearing. I wanted him to take responsibility for his actions, and he eventually did, but I would have forgiven him even if he hadn't admitted his wrong. His father...? I know I said at the State Bar hearing that I had not forgiven him, but I felt such a release and peace afterwards, that I knew I had forgiven him.

Cole and I, and his dad and mom and my family share one terrible moment in time and are bound together because of it. The Sorensons are not bad people. Like us all, they are trying to find their way, and if God forgives them, how can I not? If God *loves* them, how can I not?

*   *   *

Ricky's death was unbearable. No parent should have to bury a child. It's unnatural. With God's help, I accepted his death, and if nothing else tragic happened in my lifetime, I would have suffered more than most— but there was more to come.

Before I take you on that harrowing voyage across dark oceans, I'm going to tell you about the life that shaped me, and the gifts I received, for those gifts gave me the will to live, to love, to laugh, and to seek joy again.

Chapter 18

The Preacher's Daughter

I am a preacher's daughter.

You may chuckle at the thought because of the way preachers' daughters are depicted in movies. The image that comes to mind is that of a child with a sour, turned-down mouth, who wears long black dresses, tight shoes, and her hair in a bun, someone who at all times tells the truth, never does anything bad, and has no fun. If that's what you think, then you haven't been a preacher's daughter. I was a good kid, but a holy terror, with an emphasis on *holy*.

Some kids suck their thumbs. With me it was fingers. As a youngster, I sucked two fingers, only two, and it didn't matter which two. My hand was sopping wet. My mother tried to stop me. She poured Tabasco sauce on them, but when her back was turned I offered my goopy fingers to the cat. Why wouldn't a cat like hot sauce?

Frustrated, my mother snatched a knife from the drawer and laid it across my fingers, threatening to cut them off if I didn't stop. I screamed, "No, no, no..." Nowadays, no one would threaten amputation as a cure for finger sucking. Then it didn't seem an unusual method for disciplining a child, and I ran away and hid. Scared as I was, it didn't stop me, and my fingers were always soggy. To my chagrin, I was, years later, blessed with a daughter who did the same thing.

I was a deceitful child. That's right, the preacher's daughter lied a lot. I didn't like egg yokes, or boiled eggs. I made my sister Gaile eat them and told her she'd be in trouble if she didn't. I hated milk, and to solve that problem, I coerced my other sister Terrie into drinking my milk. When she wasn't cooperative, I poured the milk down the sink. Once, my mother caught me pouring milk into the trash can, and I got it good.

I felt guilty about telling lies and would go to church, kneel at the altar and ask God to forgive me. I don't even know why I lied. Maybe it was a reaction to having to be good all the time, being controlled and under control. Like when we visited people's homes. My mom wanted us to be perfectly groomed. Our clothes were clean and starched. We weren't allowed to ask for things. If we were eating, we couldn't ask for seconds, and had to say, "Yes Ma'am," "Yes Sir," "No Sir." My parents were strict and told us to sit down and not wiggle.

Perhaps I was rebelling. I was in trouble constantly, and my mother repeated the age old threat, "When your father gets home..." My father spanked me when I deserved it and seemed more distressed than I was. I tried to be good so he wouldn't suffer.

I should clarify that when I was born and during my finger-sucking and lying stages, I was not yet a preacher's daughter. That came later. I started life in Logansport, Indiana, on February 24, 1957, as Sharon Veneita Rushing. I was the daughter of a man in the U.S. Air Force, a helicopter mechanic who flew rescue missions.

There were five children in my family. Ande was born in 1954, Bill in 1955, Terrie in 1960, and Gaile in 1962. I was the middle child. As an Air Force family, we moved around a lot. I remember being on an airplane flying back from Guam, I was almost three, and the Easter Bunny bounced up and down the aisles handing out Easter baskets. My mother says I can't possibly remember that, but I do.

I remember the town of Valdosta, Georgia. We lived in a trailer park, and had a Lassie dog named Jim, who got in a fight, and had a mane like a lion during the summer because we shaved him, and I played in his doghouse. I turned the hose on under our trailer to make mud pies, and convinced my brothers to eat them. Today people say I can convince anybody of anything.

Everybody said I was dad's favorite and when I was little, my siblings often whispered, "Go ask dad, he'll let you do it." I admit he let me do almost anything I wanted, and I worshipped the ground he walked on, but I don't want to make him into too much of a hero here. My dad was not standing in line for sainthood. Not then.

When my father was a teenager, he was involved with the church and felt the Lord had called him to the ministry. But after he joined the Air Force, he stopped attending church, and strayed. He drank and smoked, and didn't live a Christian life. He had red hair and a temper to go with it. He'd fought a lot when he was a kid, nobody messed with my dad, and he was a no nonsense kind of dad when we were growing up. He could be fun when we went places, but you did not want to make him mad. Even though I never saw him in a rage, I was told he had an explosive temper.

When I was five, my father left the military, and we moved to Memphis, Tennessee, where things improved for us financially. He worked for the Hyster Company, which made forklifts, and then Dupont, which seemed to make everything else in the world. We moved from a mobile home trailer into a three-bedroom brick house, which to us was like a mansion.

Gifts My Father Gave Me

We lived in a new subdivision up on a hill and behind our house was a grove of trees we called the jungle where we played Tarzan and Jane. In summer, Memphis was hot, humid, and buggy, and the grass was emerald green. In winter, we had ice storms, and when it snowed we built snowmen and igloos, and sledded down the hill. Because the snow was wet, we wore plastic baggies on our hands and feet. In grade one, I learned to ride a bike, but hadn't learned how to brake, and in order to stop would deliberately smash into neighbors' bushes.

My mom took us kids to church. My dad was too busy working. If he wasn't at his job, he was rebuilding motors for extra income, and that included Sundays, except for the time his friend, Forrest McCullough, who he'd grown up with, visited our area to preach at a real southern revival. We lived in the Bible Belt, and the revival services ran for a week and featured speakers and singers.

The night Forrest spoke, my mom stayed home with my siblings who had the chicken pox, and I was the only one to go with my dad to the Memphis First Church of the Nazarene, an old southern church with big white columns and a hundred and fifty steps leading up to its entrance.

This church service was not like anything we'd ever seen. At our church, we were used to scholarly preachers, ordered singing, and peaceful prayer. Here people were praying out loud and shouting—

Hallelujah! Praise the Lord!

—which, if you hadn't heard it before, is frightening to a child.

During the service, the minister invited anyone who wished to accept Jesus as their Savior to leave their seats and come down to pray at the altar. My dad didn't go, and at one point Forrest stepped away from the altar, tromped down the aisle, and stopped in front of us.

"Don't you want to get your heart right with the Lord?" he said, close enough to my dad's face that he could have kissed him.

I grabbed my dad's arm, and pleaded, "Don't do it, don't do it!" Because I was scared, I was five-years-old, I didn't understand what they wanted him to do.

"Not tonight," my dad said.

Relieved, I let out a sigh. But I felt something was up. My dad was clutching the back of the pew and his knuckles were white. The service continued and they sang the invitation again, *Just As I Am...* Then the pastor, Bro Beckum, rattled down the aisle, threw his arms around my dad, and said, "Red, don't you want to give your life to Christ?" They called my dad Red then.

"Not tonight," he repeated.

Forrest McCullough returned to my dad's side and said, "Andrew, we're not leaving until you're safe in the Kingdom."

Finally, my dad surrendered the pew, rose, and with my arms wrapped tightly around his leg, dragged me to the front of the church along with him. He knelt at the altar, and they beat on his back with the palms of their hands and shouted—

Hang on...

Hang on...

Gifts My Father Gave Me

People in the congregation bellowed—

Let go, let go, let go...

I didn't know what was going on, and as they gathered around my father, I shook with terror. He was praying real hard at the altar, and everyone in the church was praying real loud. I felt a tap on my shoulder. A kid asked if I wanted to go with him. I sure didn't want to be where I was.

He led me outside and we ran up and down the one hundred and fifty steps, up and down, up and down, playing tag, which my mother never would have allowed, and that's how, while I was playing and he was praying, my dad renounced his bad ways, gave his life back to God and eventually became a preacher like he said he would when he was a young boy.

The transition to preacher was not quite that fast, even though it seemed that way to me, and took some time to evolve. After that night when he gave himself to the Lord, he quit smoking and seemed a lot happier. He didn't have a bad temper anymore. He started teaching Sunday School, and when the preacher was busy, my dad filled in for him in small churches way out in the country in Tennessee, Arkansas or Mississippi.

On one occasion, he was asked to fill in for a preacher who had to go out of town. I think this was my dad's tenth sermon, and early that Sunday morning, the seven of us piled into our station wagon, and drove to the church to hear my dad preach. There were twenty-five people in attendance, and he delivered the sermon like he was addressing a thousand. His voice boomed, and flames shot from his blue eyes. Maybe I'm exaggerating, but with his red hair, dimpled chin, and commanding presence, you would have thought he was on fire.

I was proud of him, and after we got back in the car, he said, "Now, I preached a long time today."

"Seven minutes," said my mother.

"I preached the whole Bible," he said. "It had to be longer than seven minutes."

"It's okay," I said. "It seemed a whole lot longer than that."

Everybody laughed, even my dad. I was his best fan. Still am.

My mom then corrected his grammar. He had a tenth grade education and sometimes messed things up. "You don't say, They *is*, you say, They *are*..." After that, when he preached, she took notes and corrected him on the way home. He accepted the criticism without rancor, the same way you tolerate the dentist's Novocain needle to numb your tooth. You don't want it, it hurts, but in the long run it's good for you.

Soon my dad was preaching regularly, and was invited to be the full-time pastor at a church in Forrest City, Arkansas. He was working at Dupont in Memphis, and decided to do both jobs. We had to give up our big house and move to Arkansas because the preacher and his family were required to live in the parsonage, a house next door to the church.

My dad drove from Forrest City to work in Memphis, then back to Forrest City, a distance of seventy miles both ways, almost every day. Then at night he called on people of the church, and preached on Sundays. After a year of this, he was preaching one Sunday night and his knees buckled. He fell to the floor and passed out.

"You can't burn yourself out like this," the doctor at the hospital told him. "You have to either quit preaching or give up your job."

My mom and dad had quite a discussion that night. He was making over $200 a week at Dupont, a lot of money in 1966. The church offered him $25 a week. He didn't qualify for a military pension, having been in the Air Force only eight years, and had nothing to supplement his income. That $25 would be our main income, besides whatever he earned as a handyman or from fixing motors.

My mom reacted like most mothers protecting their young. She wailed that we were going to starve to death. I was in third grade, but understood what starving to death meant, and did not like the idea. My father replied that when he chose to serve the Lord, he agreed not to hold anything back.

"I feel like the Lord's calling me to preach full-time," he said.

"Are you crazy?" said my mom. "You've got a tenth-grade education, you don't even have good grammar. And you have five kids to support. If this is what you were thinking of doing, you should have done it from the start. Now it's too late."

"The Lord is calling me," he responded.

My mom is strong in her faith, and calm in the way she approaches things. But she knew we couldn't live on that salary. My father's never been fearful, and didn't mind stepping into the unknown. He accepted the Lord's call, gave up his job, and became the preacher. My mom called him an idiot. She's a realist, and maybe she was right about my father being an idiot, but if he was an idiot, then I loved idiots. This idiot got me my own room.

The parsonage was a sweeping yellow brick ranch-style with two bathrooms and five bedrooms, two on the main level and three in the basement. And one of the basement bedrooms was entirely mine. It was the first time I'd had my own bedroom. And I was only eight. How cool is that?

Of course, I was too young to grasp the long-term implications of my dad becoming a full-time preacher.

The church owned the parsonage and it was compulsory that the pastor live there. He couldn't plan for retirement, he couldn't buy a home and build equity for his family. Some churches have changed their attitude, and now provide a living allowance, but back then the rule stood.

Not only that, my dad was required to look after the place. He did everything from changing light bulbs to raking leaves to repairing the roof of the parsonage and the church. Volunteers helped out now and then, but the pastor was responsible for the maintenance as well as for visiting sick parishioners, preparing sermons, giving services, helping with programs, looking after his own family, and doing other jobs to make ends meet. He was ministering, writing, preaching, helping, repairing, building, visiting, counseling, teaching, praying... It's a job you did only if God wanted you to, because you couldn't do it on your own strength or you'd become a crazy person.

As if he wasn't busy enough, my father went back to school. He failed English, but they passed him anyway because they were flabbergasted that my dad had five kids, was a preacher with a congregation to tend, and had the gumption and willpower to improve himself. My father eventually became a good student, but it took him a long time.

To this day, he is a poor reader. If you hear him read, you think, *Holy Cow*, what did he say? My mom made him practice reading the Bible aloud, and often said, "You slaughter the Scripture." You may wonder, How could he go into the ministry? I think God gave him a gift to understand Scripture. He makes it make sense, he makes it relevant and practical.

My father eventually went on to earn a degree in theology and a master's degree in value engineering, which is taking existing facilities and changing them to accommodate your needs. He actually helped write the correspondence course for the University of Wisconsin. He's a talented man, but more than that, he never gives up. Even if he wanted to, I don't think the Lord would let him.

Sacrificing a good paying job for preaching caused a huge lifestyle change for my mom. They'd saved before he became a pastor, but soon the money dwindled and was gone. I often heard her complain about the lack of money, but in this case she had a point. She and my dad argued about finances constantly, yet if you ask my dad, he will tell you that mom stood behind him.

It was a huge lifestyle change for me, too. A good one. The house was situated on a hill, and my brothers and sisters and I rolled through the tall grass down the hill, and then tottered across a fallen tree that traversed a ravine behind the house. We stalked squirrels, rabbits and snakes, and rode a horse named Queenie and a pony called Cochise. Ande and Bill made poles and practiced pole vaulting for track at school.

The lifestyle change was not all fun and horseback rides, however. I had become, without anybody asking my permission, the preacher's daughter, and no longer had a private life, which was okay with me, I didn't mind. At the age of eight I wasn't a private person. Maybe that's a scary idea for most children, but not for me because life was simple: My dad said it was *okay* to live in a glass house, so it was. Like most children, whatever daddy said I believed. When I was sick, he sat on the bed beside me and told me my headache would go away, and it did. If he said something, it was like God saying it. That gave me tremendous confidence, and it was okay with me if I was a preacher's daughter. I knew who I was.

As the preacher's daughter, I was aware that I was on display. Everybody criticizes and evaluates what the preacher's kids do. I was expected to live a step above and a step under. My values and actions had to be beyond reproach, and my style of living had to be modest.

Modest is the first cousin to *poor*. With my father's meager salary, it was no problem. Poverty was supposed to be next to godliness, and people expected the preacher to live in poverty. For some reason, which I can't fathom, being destitute and one step away from standing in line at a soup kitchen made you sincere with God.

People expected us to somehow live better, but with lots less. In other words, we didn't have much money or resources, but we were expected to be the smartest, and the best behaved, and maybe not the poorest, but definitely living hand-to-mouth with nothing to spare. I suppose that kept us humble.

I was good at humble. Like the time my mom and grandmother bought us new clothes for Easter. I got a new dress, and everything matched, the dress, the shoes, the gloves and hat. I put on my new outfit for church, and when my father saw it, he became troubled.

"Sharon... come here and let me talk to you," he said kindly. "If there's a little girl in church that can't afford a new dress for Easter," he said, "she won't feel bad if you don't have a new dress, but if you have a new dress, then it's going to make her feel bad."

He'd asked me in a way that I felt chosen, special, that I had an opportunity to make somebody feel good. At least not feel bad. To wear one of my old dresses was not a punishment, it was a privilege, and I was never resentful when he asked me to do things like this.

Whenever we had hard times, my dad didn't describe our lives as miserable. We didn't think of ourselves as sufferers.

Gifts My Father Gave Me

We believe in what the book of James says—

Consider it all joy...

When hard times came, we regarded difficulty as a joy, because it was a chance to grow.

My mom and dad worked hard after he became a preacher, and often did without. Dad did extra work at a nearby motel because he was handy fixing refrigerators, air conditioners and broken windows. Sometimes he got paid, sometimes he didn't. I don't think he was ever paid what he was worth, but that was okay with him. He was happiest helping, and never asked for money.

Sometimes I heard my mother crying because we didn't have money for groceries, and my dad would tell her not to worry. Then one night the doorbell rang and my mom went to the door. There were twelve sacks of groceries sitting on the porch. My mom wept, and my dad said, "You know God is not going to let us starve."

Despite our financial challenges, my parents' door was open to everyone. The congregation had grown to over 200, and mom and dad entertained all the time. My mom made awesome soup. Everybody wanted to come over after church and eat my mom's food. She turned cheap food into masterpieces.

She was and still is a striking woman. Dark brown almost black hair, great high cheek bones, a wide smile and animated brown eyes. She made everyone who visited us feel comfortable and welcome. She had to learn to cook far different than what she was used to. She found new ways to use chicken and noodles and beans, and powdered milk instead of real milk. With five kids, she discovered how to prepare things that were nutritious, that filled us up, and were not expensive.

The Preacher's Daughter

Mom's fear of us starving to death didn't come true, not even close. She had other things to worry about, things on a biblical scale, like plagues. Not locusts or an infestation of frogs, but floods. Nobody told us that every time it rained the parsonage's basement would fill with six or more inches of water. Our piano was in the basement along with my bedroom, and my parents had bought me new furniture. The first time it rained, the water gushed in, and my mom grabbed the squeegee and tried to soak up the water before it did damage. I lifted my dresser and bed and shoved soup cans under the legs.

The piano was damaged, and the flood pushed my mother to new heights of rhetoric when confronting my father. *We're going to starve to death* was replaced with *You brought us to this place and our stuff is ruined, our life's savings is gone*, and she was bawling. I'm not making fun of her, I'm sure I would have felt the same way if I'd been her, saddled with five kids, no money, and a flooded basement. With my child's eyes, I saw this as an adventure.

I felt bad for my dad. I thought, Here my dad is trying to do God's bidding and my mom's complaining. I felt bad for my mom, too, seeing her scooping out the water with a pail, and pulling out boxes of clothes, shoes, and dresses from my closet, all ruined. After two years, my father installed a sump pump that allowed the water to drain. We lived in the parsonage four years, but for the first couple of years, despite having my own room, it was not fun living in the basement.

Looking back on that period of my life, if I were my mother, I would have killed my dad. I would have killed him. She's a remarkable person for letting him live.

I haven't told you the worst part about living in the basement during the floods. Sure, I slept on a bed floating on soup cans, but the worst part was the next pestilence, the plague of worms. You read that right, *worms*.

The first time I went to bed during a storm, I was dozing off when I felt something land on my face. I swished it away, and then recognized what the mushy thing was. It was a worm. I was grossed out and screamed. I turned on the light, looked up and saw an army of worms wiggling across the ceiling. From that moment on, I wore socks to bed and kept my flip-flops on top of the bed in case I had to get up in the middle of the night to go to the bathroom. The worms made that squishy bug sound when you stepped on them.

Even when it wasn't raining, the worms sometimes slithered into my room, and you never knew when they would squirm under your feet. I do confess, however, that when I wasn't screaming with revulsion, I hooted with laughter.

My mother didn't think it was funny.

Chapter 19

Like Every Other Kid

In many respects, I was like every other kid in America. I played in the yard with my brothers and sisters, climbed trees, and lay down on my back in the grass looking up at the clouds. We sat around the dining room table and ate and laughed at jokes and discussed serious matters. We watched TV, rode bikes and went shopping. Every year we embarked on a two-week vacation in a new part of the country, camped out, went swimming, roasted marshmallows, and had fun.

But there were differences in my upbringing that made me different than most kids at school. I was taught how to run a household and cook, and at times was asked to prepare lunch or dinner for company. Thanks to my mom, by the time I was in fifth grade, I could do almost anything. My mom also taught me how to clean the church, and wax the hardwood floors, and the pews. I waxed the pews so hard that people slid down in their seats.

I was as comfortable in a church as most kids are in their own living rooms. When there were no services during the week, I'd ask the neighborhood girls to bring their Barbie Dolls to the church. Other kids played house, but we played church. I was the preacher. I played the piano, and was the boss about everything. My husband says not much has changed.

Like many kids, I was taught responsibility, and wanted to work and make money. I got $5 a week cleaning the church and saved it for Christmas and bought everybody a present. I babysat my two younger sisters and took care of them, but sometimes I was a brat and made them eat soap.

"Close your eyes, stick out your tongue," I'd say. "I promise it's not soap, it's good candy."

Every time it was soap. That was the cost of having a sister as nice as me. Nevertheless, despite my momentary devilish lapses with a bar of soap, I was a respectful kid. I think it's because we knew our boundaries. Too often people brought kids to church and the kids had no discipline. They wandered around during services and made noise. Then we saw other people being too strict. My dad said, "It's not how strict or how lenient you are, it's how consistent."

My dad understood how to treat us. He didn't criticize us for something and then turn around the next day and praise us for it. He knew what anxiety and misery lurked in vacillation. My mother wondered if he took his position a step too far. We walked to the bus stop to go to school and it didn't matter if it was raining or snowing. One time someone in the church called my dad and said their car broke down and asked my dad to drive their kids to school, and he did. My mom was annoyed and said, "Why do you take their kids to school and our kids have to walk?" Consistency.

Without consistency, I wouldn't have known who I was, and I've treated my kids and grandkids the same way. They always know where they stand, what they can and can't do, without guessing or trying to figure us out.

PHOTO ALBUM

Rushing family vacation, 1963; L-R: Andrew, Bill, Terrie,
Sharon, Gaile, Ande, Dicksie

Rushing children; L-R: Ande, Terrie, Bill, Gaile, Sharon

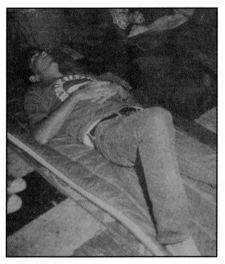

Sabetha Herald photo of Doug
snoozing on the bicycle ride,
1973

Doug and Sharon's
1st anniversary

Sharon's bicycle trip, 1973

Rushing children; L-R:
Ande, Terrie Sharon,
Gaile, Bill, Devin

Sharon and her Dad

Rushing family; L-R: Gaile, Terrie, Bill, Sharon, Dicksie,
Andrew, Ande (not pictured; Devin)

Ricky Knutson
1980
4 years old

Justin, Misty and Ricky

Ricky's last school photo

Justin and Misty, 1st photo
taken without Ricky

Ricky's last Christmas

1982 Knutson family; L-R; Ricky, Doug, Sharon, Misty, Justin

DPS Motor Officer
Doug Knutson

Sunday before Doug
was killed; L-R: Doug,
Sharon, Misty, Justin

Knutson annual
family photo

Misty's wedding

Misty and Justin

Justin's graduation from Basic Training,
Ft. Benning, GA

The Knutson-Felix blended family; L-R: David, Tina,
Sharon, Jada, Justin, Misty

David and Sharon

Deputy Director David
Felix; Department of
Public Safety

Like most fathers in America, my father wanted to prepare me for the world. But his lessons were not about finance, politics, and getting a good job. His lessons were about values. For example, he taught me tolerance. God loves us regardless of who we are and where we are in our lives. My father felt we should be as forgiving and as tolerant as God would be.

My father did not equate love with approval, or love with acceptance according to a detailed moral code. For him, love had no strings attached. He accepted people for who they were, and loved them no matter their failings or sins. One of his mottos was: If you could be as hard on yourself as you are on other people and as understanding of other people as you are of yourself, you would be a good person.

Perhaps he was harder on his children than on other people because he wanted us to reach for those high moral standards. Whichever way you look at it, we were on parade and role models and had a responsibility to behave in a certain way. Yet he forgave us when we failed, and loved us no matter what. Love was the end goal. He talked not about how you looked or behaved, but about your heart—

Did you do it with heart?
Was your heart good or bad?
Was love in your heart?

He wanted us to love others, and to serve as an example to inspire others. For instance, you know pastors don't make much money. As a courtesy, the preachers' kids were allowed to go to church camp for half price. My mom and dad wouldn't let us. We had to get a job and pay full price. Their feeling was that we should show others we were willing to pay our share.

Gifts My Father Gave Me

We didn't attend a special church school as you might expect. Like the other kids in our area, we went to the regular public elementary school. It was a small school in a small town, population around 12,000. About 500 kids went to the school, and thirty were in my class. The kids in my family were average, normal kids. We weren't weird, my brothers played sports well, and I had lots of friends.

Even so, I was different in my way of thinking. Because I was centered, I had a strong influence on other kids, and never wanted to be like anyone else. Even the rich kids... I thought, Gosh, it would be nice to be rich, but I didn't envy them. I felt that instead of me wanting to be like them, they wanted to be like me.

I knew who I was. I didn't want to be a rock star like a lot of kids today, and saw as my role models my Sunday School teacher and our youth pastor. They inspired me to excel, and to find ways to be a better person. Like at school. I was a good student at public school, number one or two in the class. I became involved in plays and was chosen for good parts. Sometimes I felt sorry for the kids who got the bad parts, and asked the teacher to let them take my roles. I was competitive, yet kindhearted. I didn't want to win at the expense of hurting others.

My father taught me to be aware of other people's feelings. There was a miniature golf competition one day and a battle between the guy who owned a local motel and my dad. The whole town was there, and when the guy was putting, I said under my breath, "Miss it, miss it."

"Sharon, don't say that," said my dad.

"I want you to win."

"Just hope I get it in less strokes, not that he misses. You don't want him to do bad. You want me to do better."

Because of my dad, that was the path I followed when I was growing up. I wanted to do better than other people, but never wanted them to do badly.

Another lesson my father taught me was about peace. I was the peacemaker child, the diplomat. Like if my brothers were arguing, I'd try to work out a compromise. I could see both sides and bring everybody together. Like my dad, I wanted to fix problems. But he taught me that you can't rush in to fix other people's problems. First you have to earn the right to help and comfort people by spending time with them, by becoming a friend, and by being nonjudgmental.

"You don't have to agree with them to love them," my father said. "You hurt with them, you cry with them, you share with them, but it's not your job to change their beliefs or to change them."

When I was a child, my father taught me I don't have to judge people, and as a result my love for people is stronger knowing that we are all humans.

I feel lucky to have the parents I do. Not many people have parents like mine and the opportunities and childhood I was provided with. There's sadness and sickness and perversion in the world, and I grew up understanding and forgiving, and appreciating that I've lived a privileged life, and do what I can to help others.

Despite feeling that I had a typical upbringing, I know I was brought up differently than most. Most people are not taught that their most important role in life is helping other people. And most people don't go to church camp. If you went to scout camp, you'd spend time working on your badges, learning to tie knots, folding flags, and canoeing. Church camp was like that, too. We had volleyball competitions, canoe races and the things you'd expect at regular camp.

At church camp, we also went beyond physical games and focused on our hearts and souls. We had services

Gifts My Father Gave Me

in the morning or at night, sometimes both, a Bible lesson in the morning, and a speaker in the afternoon. We learned Scriptures, and studied stories in the Old Testament, like the book of Ruth, and the book of Esther, and the story about Joseph and his coat of many colors. Many of the camp instructors made the Bible live for us. They helped us grasp the concepts easily, and it was an awakening experience. The basic idea behind church camp was to reinforce not so much who we were, because few teens know, but who God is and our relationship with Him.

Lest I make it sound too perfect and unbelievably virtuous, church camp was also about who was popular and who was not. Every year the camp voted for a king and queen. My brother Bill was crowned one year, and it's no wonder. He was a popular kid, the class clown, and fun to be with. He looked like the all-American boy with pale blue eyes, curly brown hair, freckles, and a big smile.

But the contest took a surreal turn when I was in fifth grade. My brother's girlfriend and I were nominated for camp queen halfway through camp, and the two of us had to fight it out to the last day when everybody would vote. My brother, who was about a year and a half older than me, and was supposed to look after his younger sister, campaigned for his girlfriend against me. Can you believe that?

As if that wasn't nervy enough, my mother wanted me to turn down the nomination. She was my camp counselor, and thought if I won it might look like she had something to do with it. She worried this would have the appearance of playing favorites. I was the pastor's daughter, she was the pastor's wife, and she was on camp staff. She knew how that looked and how gossip started, and wanted to protect me.

Like Every Other Kid

Lucky for me, the camp director stepped in and told my mother she didn't have a say in the nomination because the camp staff didn't nominate me, my peers did, and on the last day of camp, I was crowned camp queen. At that moment, life didn't get much better.

Chapter 20

A Person That Matters

W hile raising the five of us, my mom and dad sometimes invited troubled kids to live with us.

We didn't have a big house, and had only one bathroom. Often we had three people in there at one time, one brushing teeth, one using the toilet and the other in the shower. Yet these kids stayed with us for several months to several years, and went to college, got married, and raised families. Over the years my dad has received letters from them saying they'd never have had a chance in life if it hadn't been for my parents who showed them that the world is big and they had a place in it.

My parents continued this practice even after I got married and left for a place of my own. A Coffeyville boy named Devin lived with his grandmother, didn't know his father, and looked up to my dad. He spent summers with my parents, and one summer when he was sixteen, my mom told him, "You're not going to live with us this summer, go home, then come back and go home again."

My parents were already paying for his school clothes and books. My mother, being a smarty, joked, "If you want to live here, tell your mother to sign the adoption papers."

His mother signed them, and he moved in. That made my mother happy. My dad was ecstatic. If it were up to him, he'd have adopted the whole world. He didn't have to do all the laundry. My mom did.

The rest of us kids happily accepted Devin into the family. We loved showing him off wherever we went, and still do. In time, Devin joined the Army and then became a firefighter in Arlington, Texas. He married a teacher, has three sons, and lives near Ande and Bill.

You may think it unusual that my parents sheltered other kids, but you have to look at my family in the context of our growing up. My dad taught us that generosity has no limits, that we must help those less fortunate than us. Kids always visited and stayed over at our house. They loved my dad, especially kids who were hurting, because my dad took an interest in them. Often we picked up kids who were underprivileged, handicapped or had no way of getting to church on their own. A girl named Dorothy lived thirty-five miles from us in a foster home. She was crippled with polio and my dad picked her up on Sunday morning and took her home after church or brought her to our place where she was surrounded by other children.

Another kid had been set on fire by someone in her family. She didn't have hair and her face was disfigured. When she showed up at school the first time, she sat by herself and nobody talked to her. I sat beside her and talked to her, hoping the other kids would do the same. They didn't. When we brought her to our place, kids treated her like she was one of us.

One of the kids my parents helped became my boyfriend. I was thirteen in Corsicana, and George came home from school with my brother Ande. He didn't wash his hair or take showers, and my mom told him, "If you come here, you have to shower."

She ordered him to take off his clothes at once and she washed them. His parents were divorced and he lived with his sister in a dirty home. My mom thought cleanliness was godliness, and lifted everybody up to her standards. Soon George brought his clothes over regularly and mom washed them. She bought him shampoo and deodorant and he looked and smelled wonderful. He lived with us off and on for months.

George eventually went to college, became a coach and teacher and did well in life. And I can think of ten other kids like George whose lives changed for the better because of my parents.

My parents taught me many lessons, generosity being only one. They taught me that hard work is a value, and that to earn your own way makes you a worthwhile human being. I've worked ever since I can remember. I babysat when I was younger for 50 cents an hour, and when I became fourteen I got my first job working at S&H Crest Company, a dime store. As I wasn't old enough to be on the payroll, the manager paid me out of petty cash. I did everything—stocked shelves, cleaned up, sold clothes and sundries, and worked the cash register during Christmas break.

Before long, I worked at the Sonic, my favorite place, best burgers in the world. I checked the orders, made change, served drinks and food, and earned a whopping 70 cents an hour. I continued cleaning the church. In Forrest City, I earned $5 a week for cleaning. After we moved to Corsicana, I got $10 or $12 a week, and learned to be a trustworthy worker and someone everyone could depend on.

My father taught me that there was nothing I couldn't do. This gave me the confidence about who I was that made people see me as a leader, and I developed my own personal philosophy: *Let's get the job done, let's do it right, and have fun while doing it.*

It seemed that every day of my growing up was a lesson in becoming a person that mattered.

Chapter 21

Growing Pains

When I was a sophomore in the Corsicana high school, I had a friend, Deana. Her parents were older than mine and she had older brothers and sisters. I think that's why they let her do whatever she wanted.

My parents didn't pick my friends. It was up to me to choose who I wanted to spend time with. That didn't stop my mother from telling me who she didn't care for, and she didn't like Deana. She thought she wasn't held accountable for what she did and was a bad influence on me.

My mother was careful about who I spent the night with—Deana could stay overnight at our place, but I was not allowed to stay at her place. Because my mom didn't trust her. It turned out my mom was right.

One Sunday night I went to church with Deana and her boyfriend and a friend of theirs, a boy visiting for the weekend from another town. I thought I was very grown-up. I was fifteen and the friend was nineteen. After church, we went to the Sonic for burgers, and then drove into the country in their truck, and the friend was at the wheel. It was getting dark, and I told everyone I had to be home by nine.

"Well, why do you gotta be home by nine?" this guy

Gifts My Father Gave Me

said. "Are you a baby?"

"It's a school night and my parents want me home early," I said.

He kept making fun of me, and then we stopped on a deserted road. Deana and her boyfriend were making out in the backseat, and this guy who I'd just met flicked the car light off. I wanted to talk, but he put his arm around me, and tried to kiss me. He'd been smoking and reeked of tobacco, and I turned my face away. He was a big guy, and grabbed and pawed me, and broke my necklace and a button on my dress. I became frightened and said, "Let's go home, take me home. Deana, I want to go."

"Oh, come on, Sharon," she said.

"Take me home," I said again.

"What's wrong?" she said, annoyed with me.

He squeezed the inside of my leg hard. I was wearing the dress I wore to church, and he tore it. I yelled, "Take your hands off me!"

I thought he was going to rape me, but I fought him off, grabbed the door handle, and bailed out. I took off down the dark road. I knew the way home, I could see lights in the distance, but we'd driven a long ways out, and I was scared.

I stumbled down the road about a quarter mile when I heard the truck start up, and I ducked down and hid in the bushes. For awhile they cruised up and down the road shouting my name. I wasn't sure what I was afraid of more, being out in the country at night or them.

They finally spotted me, and Deana hung out of the cab and yelled, "Sharon, we'll take you home. He won't bother you, you can sit by me."

I stepped back on the road and got in the truck, and sat against the door in the back. Well, they didn't take me home, they dropped me off at Darlene's, a friend from church. She helped me get cleaned up as much as I could, and I called my parents to say I'd be home soon.

Darlene drove me home, and I was crying. What are my mom and dad going to say? I thought. Look at my hair, look at my face, and my clothes... He'd roughed me up, and my first instinct was to tell my dad. I knew my mom would have a fit. She'd told me Deana was not a nice girl. I was too young, and shouldn't have been out with her and her friends. I was smarter than that. He hadn't raped me, but I felt sick and violated and out of control. I knew people would blame me for it, and I was responsible.

I walked into the house, and my mom asked me where I'd been. I said I had been at Deana's and then went to Darlene's. "Why did you go to Darlene's?" she said.

I burst out crying. My brother Ande came in then and my dad said, "What's wrong?"

"I thought he was going to rape me," I blurted out.

My mom was about to say something when my dad told her to let me be. He led me into the other room and we sat down.

"Tell me what happened," he said.

"It's Deana's friend. We went riding, and then out into the country."

My dad didn't accuse me of anything. He didn't say, "What did you do?" He said, "Tell me what he did."

"He broke my necklace and ripped the front of my dress." I showed him the bruises on my legs, I had marks all over my legs. Ande got mad, and said he was going to beat the guy up.

My dad was mad too. Not at me, at the guy. Then he gave me some advice. "That's why you don't go out with older guys," he said. "They take things differently. You might be innocent, you might be acting cute and funny, but they think you are being seductive."

My dad said that if I had been raped, he hoped I

would have come to him immediately. He said one of the most disappointing things for him would be if I didn't tell him about being raped or getting pregnant.

"I would love you more if you came to me," he said, "and I'd help you through anything, even if it's not what I want to do."

In his counseling, he dealt with situations of every sort, and I think the most important thing he wanted to convey was that he would love me no matter what happened.

I made a bad choice with this guy, but that didn't give him the right to hurt me. After I told what happened, my brother jumped in the car and went over to Deana's place, and had it out with the guy who swore he didn't hurt me. He told my brother that I was hot stuff, which was not a clever thing to say to the brother of a girl you manhandled.

When my brother got home, he told my father what he'd said to the guy, which included a four-letter word. My father laughed heartily. We never used profanity in our house. To hear it leap out of my brother's mouth was extremely funny. I was also shocked that my father laughed. It must have been from stress.

Ande didn't beat the guy up, but he grabbed him and threatened him. He told him to never come back to our town again. The guy said, "I'm leaving now," ran out to his truck and took off. Ande was smaller than this guy, but I'm certain my brother could be mean when he's defending his little sister.

You have to understand Ande. He was far from being a violent person. He was an athlete, singer, actor, church youth leader, and popular with the girls. He has deep green eyes and brown hair, and I was in awe of him. For him to stick up for me like that made me love him all the more, and I regret feeding him mud pies when we were kids. As penance, I sent him my baby-sitting money after he went to college.

I look back on the attempted rape now and think, how brainless. I could have been seriously hurt. My parents had given me the tools, spiritual, psychological, and practical, to prevent me from getting into a situation like that, but I had ignored everything I'd learned.

At that time, my dad was commuting from Corsicana to Bethany, Oklahoma, to attend college. He'd leave on Sunday night after church and attend school Mondays and Tuesdays and then would drive home Tuesday night. He rode a motorcycle because it was cheaper.

After I told my dad about the attempted rape, he asked if I'd like to go to Bethany with him the next day. I would get out of school for two days, I was going with my dad on the back of a motorcycle, I had friends I could visit while dad was in school. It was not a hard decision.

We set out on the motorcycle and I hugged him from behind all the way and thought, The world is safe. We had a wonderful two days, me and my dad, and then headed home, and on the way, stopped at a truck stop. My dad went to the bathroom, and after he came out, we sat down at a picnic table. He took two small, square wrappers, which he probably got from a machine in the bathroom, from his pocket. He handed them to me and said, "Do you know what these are?"

"I have no idea," I mumbled, wishing I could hide behind a tree. I didn't want to lie to my dad, but I was very embarrassed. I knew what they were. My brothers weren't sexually active, but they'd bought some condoms, showed them to me and told me what they were for.

The condoms my dad bought were sitting on the picnic table at the truck stop and people were passing by our table. I was afraid they'd see them, but my dad closed his hand around them. He then described what they're used for, what they're good for, and why sometimes they're not good.

He asked if I was sure Ande or Billy hadn't said anything about them because he'd talked to them about sex. I gulped and said, "No." I'm sure he told them not to say anything to me because mom was intending to have the *birds and the bees* talk with me. A lot of parents don't talk about sex, it's a hush-hush subject. If the subject came up, my mom would blush and leave the room. My dad wasn't that way at all.

"Sex is the most beautiful thing in the world," he said.

He told me that condoms can prevent pregnancy, but they might have holes in them and leak. "If you buy them," he said, "then you've made the first step to having sex, but sex is not what it's about. It's about love."

He said that sex outside of marriage was wrong, and I should wait until I was married, and enjoy it, and then I'd understand what sex and loving mean. I was thinking, I don't want to talk to my dad about this. But it was okay listening. Then he asked what my mom told me about sex. I laughed. I was nervous. When I was in fifth or sixth grade, a package arrived in the mail, and my mom handed it to me after school and told me to go to my room and open it. "If you have any questions," she said, "you can ask me later."

Inside the package were three books on growing up, menstruation, and everything you were afraid to ask about sex and the female body. You think I would ask my mom a question about condoms and sex? No way. I'd ask my brothers. Well, that was the extent of our mother-daughter talk. She said that after I read the books I should put them on the top shelf of my closet and they'd be there for me when I needed them.

Sitting at the truck stop, I told my dad about the box and the books, and he chuckled. He didn't know my mom had given them to me. I think he thought she would have talked to me a little.

Talking to my dad was a nurturing experience. Instead of yelling at me, "You failed, you screwed up, you're done for," he used this opportunity to teach me something.

When I got married, Doug and I were in the car about to leave on our honeymoon, and my dad stuck his head in the driver's window, leaned over, kissed me good-bye and said, "There's one thing I want you guys to know."

Oh, oh, I thought. What's he going to say?

"The Scriptures say the marriage bed is undefiled," he said. "Whatever two people do when they're married, what they feel comfortable consenting to, is their business. Sex is a gift from God, and I want you to have a good life."

Doug was impressed. What father-in-law would have the courage to share his insight and knowledge about a risky subject like sex?

After our honeymoon, from time to time my dad would casually bring up the subject. He didn't lecture us or suddenly say, "Hey, how's your sex life?" He told us stories from his counseling sessions. That way it was less threatening, and we were open to listening. "I counseled this lady in the church..." was how he often began, (no names were used), and it wasn't a long, drawn-out talk. It was short and simple. It was his way of teaching and it worked. He could turn something negative into something wonderful and helpful.

It did backfire on me, however. Doug liked discussing things with my dad and when we had issues, he would often say, "Let's call your dad."

"No, don't call my dad," I often responded. "He's not your dad. He's my dad, and I'll talk to him."

Chapter 22

Motors

After Ricky died, the days slid by, each day a challenge to get out of bed, get dressed, put one foot in front of the other, and live a life *without*.

My life went on. Doug went to work, Misty and Justin went to school, we went to church, we went away for holidays, we visited our parents, we learned to experience joy again and the ordinary things of life, while the music of Ricky's life played low and continuous in the background. His first tooth, his first word, his first laugh. Many, many firsts...

As I went about my daily routine, talking on the phone, shaking hands, driving the car, laughing at jokes, crying at the movies—his life came to me in brief musical interludes, and as time advanced, the interludes became shorter and shorter until I could hear only a few notes at a time, and then I began to forget the funny things he had said, the warmth of his face, the sweet odor on his clothes, his gleeful smile. I forgot the song in his voice.

As the years passed in a jumble, the music wound down and eventually stopped and all that remained was the quietness of *gone*. He was in God's good hands now, I had nothing to fear, and the throbbing sadness was replaced with simply longing. As his absence grew in me, the burden I carried grew less and less until I no longer shouldered the weight of *Why did it happen? Why wasn't I there? Why couldn't I save him?*

The Lord helped me through it all, but *gone* is a very long time.

Ricky died in 1983, and Doug and I found it hard to go on. We didn't want to work, or do much of anything. But after about a year, we swam the river of tears to the other side. Doug continued to lay carpet, and soon went to work for the owner of a carpet store. I started attending Scottsdale Community College. With the money from Ricky's accident settlement, we paid off our debts and bought a house in Phoenix, Arizona. Odd how Ricky's death benefited us. It wounded our hearts, but made us solvent.

Doug was on his way to work one day when a police officer wearing tall black leather boots and a starched uniform rumbled by on his motorcycle. Doug had ridden motorcycles as a kid, and for fun we frequently went on motorcycle trips. He thought, Why not mix fun with work? It was a nice idea, but Doug hated taking tests, and put it out of his mind.

Then fate stepped in. The Department of Public Safety (DPS) was recruiting at the college where I was going to school, and I picked up an application form. Without telling Doug, I filled it out, and mailed it off. Sometimes you have to light a flame to the rocket under somebody else's dreams. Was he surprised when DPS called him to come down to the department to take a battery of tests including written, physical, medical, hearing, drug screening, polygraph, and psychological. Fortunately, he passed every step.

DPS soon sent an officer to our house to conduct a background investigation.

"What I really want to do is ride motors," Doug told the officer who was interviewing him.

Motors, at that time, had a bad reputation. The motor cops were cocky, independent thinkers, and didn't play well with others. They weren't team players.

"Don't tell anybody you want to be in motors," said the guy who was clearly not fond of motor cops, "or you'll never get anywhere."

Doug couldn't see himself doing anything else. When he told his best friend, Dave Platt, a DPS officer who was not a motor cop, what he wanted to do, Dave replied, "Why do you want to be a butthead?"

Doug hadn't looked at it that way before.

After completing the police academy, Doug started out in DPS and was told that if he wanted to be a real highway patrolman, he had to get out of the city and work a rural area in a patrol car. They said it was a better training ground. Consequently, we moved to Salome, Arizona, for a year.

Life was different after the move. We lived in a double-wide trailer in a small retirement community. It was half the size of our home in Phoenix, but we managed to cram everything we owned into it. For a few days a week I commuted to college in Phoenix, 135 miles one way. I'd taken up jogging with Doug when he was in the police academy, and after we moved, I continued running about three to four mornings a week. Run to the post office, pick up the bills, and walk back.

Both Misty and Justin adjusted well, and did fine in school. Justin was in third grade, and Misty in second.

Misty became *Miss Socialite of Salome* and made friends with most of the older couples in our community. She reminded me of me. She was full of energy and didn't show signs of long-term trauma as a result of witnessing Ricky's death. She eventually grew her thick, dark brown hair past her shoulders. As an adult, she's about my height. Her big eyes are brown, green and hazel. She has beautiful long eyelashes, her smile and laugh are contagious, and her voice is warm and golden. No wonder everyone likes her.

Justin would in time grow into a tall, thin kid with broad shoulders. He played baseball and was nick-named *The Natural*. This from a sickly kid who was not expected to live. He had light brown hair, until he decided during his sophomore year of high school to shave his head. He was very strong, and with piercing blues eyes, long eyelashes, intimidating stare and cue-ball head, he frightened some people. He eventually joined the Army. Appearances aside, Justin is a sweet, sensitive guy, even though he wants people to think he is as tough as a cast-iron frying pan.

Although we had moved to a new town, I couldn't move away from thoughts of Ricky. On occasion, he entered my dreams. Since he was the oldest child, I always thought of him as bigger than Justin and Misty. One night in a dream, I saw the three kids running across a field to the house. I saw Justin and Misty as the seven and eight year olds they were, and for the first time Ricky looked smaller than they were. After that, Ricky stayed six in my dreams and the other kids grew older and bigger.

Years later, we went to Ricky's high school graduation. It wasn't really his graduation, it should have been, but it was that of his friends. It was hard for us to see them getting on with their lives. While sitting in the auditorium, Doug and I cried and talked about Ricky. We wondered, What would Ricky be like? What would our lives be like had he lived?

After a year in Salome, Doug transferred to Phoenix, and I was happy to move back into our house. The commutes to school were exhausting.

For the next two years, Doug worked *The Ditch* in a patrol car. That's what they called the I-17 that meandered through Phoenix. It had high concrete walls on both sides, and looked like it was down in a ditch. During the summer, with temperatures sometimes exceeding 120 degrees, the ditch radiated the intense heat onto the roadway, and everyday Doug soaked his uniform with sweat.

Finally, after three years in DPS, Doug was allowed to be a motor cop. I watched Doug prepare for his first day as a motor officer. He put on a crisp, tight uniform, yanked on the long black leather boots he admired, thrust his hands into the gloves, and slung a leg over his bike. He cranked the engine to a roar, and grinned. His eyes sparkled and he was his dream, a motor cop, butthead or otherwise. It was the first time I saw Doug happy since Ricky was killed five years earlier.

When Doug became a motor, there was hostility between motor cops and cruiser cops. Sometimes it was friendly rivalry, sometimes not. When motors arrested somebody and had to transport him to jail, they'd call for a car, and often got hassled. The attitude of the cruiser cops was, *If you catch 'em, you clean 'em*—you take the bad guy to jail, if need be on the back of your bike.

Doug ignored the antagonism and assisted the cruiser cops at accident scenes. He helped change the image of the swaggering motor officers and everyone liked and respected him. Then, much to my amazement, after three years in motors, Doug suddenly quit and joined the governor's security detail. He loved motorcycles, but the new detail was a prestigious job that put his career on the fast track to promotion. The job was like the Secret Service, and he was responsible for looking after the governor of the state.

Although Doug traveled a great deal and worked a lot of hours, Arizona Governor Fife Symington didn't live too far from our house, and Doug and I and the kids could have breakfast together in the morning and he could be at work in five minutes. On Sundays, the governor often didn't go anywhere early in the morning, and the detail guys hung out at our house and talked, drank coffee, read the paper, or attended church with us until they were called out.

Nevertheless, the lure and prestige of the governor's office wore off fast. "I feel like a babysitter," Doug said. "It's not what I joined for."

Doug was a cheerful guy, but began to hate going to work. He wasn't having fun and missed motors. He left the security detail after a year and a half, and joined Criminal Investigations (CI). Maybe Doug hated the governor job, but I loathed CI. In this position, he was a plainclothes detective and went undercover digging out drug dealers. He let his hair grow longer, wore scruffy clothes, and hung out in bars, which was a challenge for somebody who didn't drink.

No matter what he did to look like a thug, his disguise was a failure. He looked like a church-going choir boy, which is what he was. His buddies often said, "Who'd buy drugs from you?"

But many did. Bad people trusted him. Maybe it was the innocent face and engaging smile. I hated the danger of it. Mostly, I resented what he did in the bars. To convince drug dealers he was a degenerate, sometimes he had to tip nude girls to dance on his lap. Heck of a job description. When I woke up in the morning and glanced at his pillow, I felt intimidated knowing I didn't have a hard body like those dancers.

Then one day he was down at DPS in his grungy undercover clothes getting gas, and one of the motors zoomed up on his motorcycle. The bike displayed new emblems, it shimmered in the sun, the guy looked pressed and clean like a superhero, and that was it for Doug.

No more grubby clothes, no more dark, smoky bars. When he got home, he said, "I'm going back to motors." I was overjoyed.

The following Monday, he put in a request to the department asking to return to motors. His friends told him he was crazy, he'd never get promoted to sergeant.

"For three years, I was in motors," he told his friends, "and it went by like three weeks. For eighteen months, I was in governor's security and it felt like an eternity. I'm going back to the road. I like wearing the uniform, and I want to ride a motorcycle."

The day he rejoined motors, he rode his bike home after work and up the driveway. He was in great spirits. He told me about strolling into the station in his motor boots and uniform. He went into the squad area where they do reports, and a motor guy came up to him. Doug didn't know him and the guy said, "New to motors?"

"Not really," said Doug, and introduced himself.

"Doug Knutson?" said the guy. "I'm glad to meet you. I've heard a lot about you."

After he got home, Doug told me, "I'm a legend in my own time."

"In your own mind..." I said.

Doug was finally happy in his profession. I was happy for him, too. By this time, I'd started a wholesale car business with a partner. I was away on occasion buying cars in Michigan and selling them in Los Angeles. But I was home most of the time, and our family was doing well.

For the next five years, Doug was in motors, and got a reputation for writing tickets. You see, he had a system. He went to Taco Bell, ordered a 12-pack, stuffed them in his saddle bags, and sat in the median of the road catching speeders. He wrote a ticket, ate a taco, wrote a ticket, ate a taco. He ate a taco for every ticket

Gifts My Father Gave Me

he wrote. In 1996 alone, he conducted 1,080 violator stops, issued 578 hazardous citations, 441 speeding citations, and assisted in 220 accident investigations.

That's a lot of tacos.

Chapter 23

The Assault

One December night, an incident happened that shook us up, and foretold the future.

Justin was home from college for Christmas break, and my dad was visiting. He'd bought an old tractor in Memphis, found a buyer in Sedona, Arizona, hauled it here on the back of a trailer and parked it in our driveway. Justin volunteered to deliver it, and took off with it late in the afternoon.

I was about to leave work for the day when Justin called and said he drove part way up a hill toward Flagstaff when the transmission went out and he was stuck. Doug walked in, he'd taken the night off for us to go Christmas shopping, and said we'd go rescue Justin.

Doug hooked up a tow dolly to our truck, and we headed out. We went westbound on Washington Street and stopped at a light on 24th Street. We were in the curb lane, and there was a car on our driver's side. The light turned green and the car beside us proceeded into the intersection. Our car didn't move.

"What're you waiting on, an invitation from the governor?" I said to Doug.

"She's going to run the light," said Doug.

Then I saw a car on the adjacent street blow through the red light and smash into the car that a moment ago had been beside us, slamming it into the front of our truck. We were knocked around a bit, but unhurt.

"She's gonna run, she's gonna run..." Doug said.

The car that caused the accident was backing out. It drove slowly around the wreck, and then the driver floored it. Doug threw the truck into reverse and backed up a dozen feet. We cut across a gas station lot and got behind the fleeing car.

"Call 9-1-1 on the cell," Doug said, "and tell them we're chasing a hit-and-run driver northbound on 24th Street. Tell them I'm a DPS officer."

I called, delivered the information, including the car's plate numbers, and said it didn't appear there was an injury, but I wasn't sure.

The speeding driver, who we saw was a woman, was moving fast and crazy. She blew through lights and cut in and out of lanes, and we pursued her up on the sidewalk. It was fun and exciting and scary. This was what my husband did for a living?

We turned eastbound on Oak Street into a bad Phoenix neighborhood. It was dark and the driver passed cars on the right side trying to evade us, but we kept up with her. I relayed the moves to the police dispatcher. Then the driver turned a corner at Oak and 30th Street, made a sudden left into a corner house, and slammed on the brakes.

We pulled in behind her and Doug said, "Tell them our location," and he swung the truck door open to go after her.

As soon as he stepped down, he shoved his hand in his back pocket. Doug didn't have a gun on him, but he was getting out his badge to show he was the police. He never got the chance.

Six or eight guys appeared out of nowhere, and grabbed him. Then one of the guys stuck a MAC-11 submachine gun against Doug's temple, and screamed, "Say goodbye, mother... I'm gonna blow your head off."

"They've got a gun, they've got a gun," I shouted into the cell phone. "They're gonna kill him!"

"Calm down, tell me where you are," said the dispatcher.

"I already told you where. They're gonna kill him! Help us!"

Then the attackers stopped talking. Everything was quiet, a silent winter night.

I heard metal crack into metal. Clack, clack, clack... The guy was pulling the trigger, but the gun didn't go off. It was misfiring. That made him mad and they threw Doug on the ground. They stomped on him, kicked him in the head and stomach and the guy with the gun hit him with the gun barrel.

There were no driveway lights, no moon. The only illumination was from our headlights. I couldn't see well, but I didn't know how Doug could have lived through the attack.

"They're beating him to death," I yelled at the dispatcher. "I've got to help him!"

"Stay in the car," she said, "the police are coming."

Whenever there's been an emergency in my life, I've taken over, and been in complete control. Not this time. I didn't know what to do. I was paralyzed and couldn't respond. I couldn't think. I sat there watching my husband being beaten to death in front of me. Everything was happening in slow motion, like being underwater, and I could hardly raise my hand.

Our truck had tinted windows and the attackers hadn't seen me. I thought about starting up the truck, hitting the gas pedal, and crushing them under the wheels, but I'd run over Doug in the process. Even if

Doug was not in the way, I don't know if I could have done it.

I heard sirens in the distance. Quickly, four or more of the attackers vanished. Two of them continued to beat Doug.

Suddenly, the door opened, and the light burst on in the cab. It was Doug. Then a guy stuck his face in, saw me, grabbed Doug from behind and yanked him out onto the ground. I was petrified. I thought that was it, he saw me, I was dead, and Doug was too.

Unexpectedly, a spotlight lit up the truck and driveway and the men rolling around on the ground. The police helicopter screamed overhead and circled.

"Oh, God, please forgive me for everything I've ever done wrong..." I said to the dispatcher. She must have wondered if I'd gone insane. She shouted something at me I didn't understand. I couldn't see Doug anymore, and then Doug appeared and pushed himself through the open door again. He had the gun in his hand.

"Sharon, take the gun," he yelled.

The guy's arm was wrapped around Doug's neck, and Doug couldn't stand up. He jammed the gun under the brake pedal. I was too afraid to touch it. Sirens blaring in the distance broke the sounds of punching and yelling.

"We gotta get out of here," a guy shouted, and started to run. "The police are coming."

The one struggling with Doug said, "I'm not goin' without my... gun."

"Get the gun, Sharon," Doug yelled.

I couldn't move.

Then the guy let go of Doug and tried to get away, but Doug grabbed him and said, "Not now, buddy. You aren't leaving."

About six or seven Phoenix police cars screeched into the driveway and the yard, their spotlights searching everywhere. I saw a cop tackle the guy running away. Doug raised one hand with the gun in it, and shouted, "I'm a cop," and, while holding the gunman in a head-lock, threw the gun into the yard.

I saw an officer put his foot on the gun. Doug and another cop wrestled the owner of the gun to the ground, and handcuffed him.

Then the cop said to Doug, "Are you okay?"

"I think my jaw's broken," he said.

An ambulance and fire truck pulled up and while Doug headed for the ambulance, the officers pulled the hit-and-run driver from her car. She was crying, and they asked her how much she had to drink. I was still in the truck talking to 9-1-1. The dispatcher told me to stay in the truck until the police came to get me, and hung up. I couldn't see Doug. I stepped out of the truck and moved toward the cops. They were giving the way-ward driver a sobriety test, making her walk a straight line.

A couple of officers turned towards me. "Who are you? Where did you come from?" said one of the cops.

"What are you doing?" said another, and grabbed my arms.

"I was in the truck talking to the 9-1-1 operator. Where's my husband?" I said. "He's the DPS officer."

They told me he was in the ambulance. The para-medics were checking him out. Then out of the darkness Doug appeared.

"Are you okay?" I said, and yanked him into my arms.

The officers separated us, took us to different cars, and questioned us about what had happened. After-wards, I called my dad, and asked him to get Justin. My dad soon arrived and after making sure we were all right, got into the truck and drove away.

Gifts My Father Gave Me

The cops then wanted to talk to Doug and me together. Since my office was only a mile away, we went over there. For the hundredth time, I described what I saw. I said that after I heard the sirens, four of them ran away except for the two beating up Doug.

"I thought there were two guys," said Doug.

I informed him there were at least six, maybe eight. Focused on the two working him over, he had no idea there were that many. Then Doug's lieutenant and sergeant rolled up, and we told the story all over again. About one in the morning, we went to the emergency room and Doug's jaw was x-rayed. It wasn't broken. The cartilage around his jaw was torn, and it hurt for days. He was not able to chew and eat. No tacos for awhile.

We got home around 3:30 in the morning. I cried most of the night, and said repeatedly, "I thought they were going to kill you," and wondered if he was actually alive or was I dreaming.

"I'm right here," he said.

"When that man pressed the gun to your head..."

"When I felt the gun barrel, I knew it was all over."

"What were you thinking?"

"The only thing that came to mind was, 'I'll see you in a minute, Ricky.'"

"When they had you on the ground and they were kicking you in the face..."

"I thought, If I don't get up, they're going to kill me. I have to get up."

The next night, I dreamed that animals were tearing Doug apart and eating him, and I woke up around three, screaming.

"Sharon, Sharon, wake up," he said.

"I don't know what I'd do if you died," I said.

"They didn't kill me."

"What if they killed us both," I asked. "Were you ready to meet the Lord?"

"Yeah, no questions asked," he said.

"I don't think I was," I said.

A few nights later, I was lying in bed and thinking, Why didn't I ask him what I really wanted to know? When the gun was pressed to his head, was he thinking of me? Was he worried they were going to rape or kill me? I guess that was the furthest thing from his mind. He was thinking of Ricky.

And that's just as good.

Chapter 24

Doug

It was exactly two weeks after the assault, the Friday morning after New Year's Day, 1998. I was having a nightmare, the same nightmare as the night before and the night before that. As usual, it was about three in the morning, and Doug shook me. "Sharon, wake up, wake up..." he said.

"I thought they were going to kill you," I said, groggy, not quite out of the dream.

Doug wrapped his hands around my throat and said, "If you don't quit waking me up, I'm going to kill you."

We laughed and hugged each other. We couldn't get back to sleep, and talked until dawn. We had the greatest morning. We talked about the kids, the house, our jobs, our parents, the state of the union, everything. Finally, we had to get up and get ready for work.

Around ten, Doug stopped by my office on the way to traffic court. He dropped in almost everyday to raid our refrigerator. I was on the phone, and he pranced by me, yanked open the fridge, snatched a Diet Coke, and stuffed chunks of chocolate peanut clusters in each jaw. He looked like a squirrel. He was wearing his black motor gloves, and left black streaks on the fridge door. Every time he came I had to wipe them off.

Gifts My Father Gave Me

You wouldn't know that his jaw was still tender from the beating, but when it came to chocolate, he'd put up with any pain. His back was sore, too, and he planned on seeing a chiropractor later in the day. As he passed my desk, he popped the top on the soda can, took a swig with his mouth full of chocolate, waved, flashed me his officer friendly smile, and headed out the door. Through the window, I saw him lift his right leg, mount his bike like getting on a horse, rev the engine, and pull away. He loved that bike.

A few months later, I found out about a practical joke the judge pulled on Doug after he got to court that day. The judge told me this himself. He said that after Doug arrived, he, the judge, went out back where Doug parked his motorcycle, and pushed it behind a dumpster. You do not dare touch a motor officer's motorcycle. It's sacrosanct.

After Doug finished testifying, he left through the back door of the courtroom and saw his bike was gone. Apparently, everyone in the courtroom heard him say, "Oh, maaaaaan!" He ran back in, he was in his full trooper outfit, and said, "Somebody stole my bike! Call the police."

Everybody burst out laughing, and he realized the joke was on him. He was the police.

For this Christmas, Justin and Misty were home from college. Justin was nineteen and Misty eighteen, and both lived out of town. Doug and I were thrilled to have them home. It was the best Christmas present we'd ever received.

During Christmas break, Misty was filling in at a law firm that she'd worked for the year before, and Justin was at my office breaking up the asphalt on the driveway. We were going to pour concrete because whenever we worked on our cars, the extreme heat of the summer softened the asphalt and our jacks sank and got stuck.

Business was slow this time of year. I wore my grubby clothes and was spending the day cleaning the office and throwing out old files. Around noon, I went out for something to eat. I didn't feel well afterwards, and headed home. As I neared the house, my cell phone rang. It was Justin.

"Where's dad working?" he said.

"Probably on the freeway," I said, because after court he would write reports or go out on patrol.

"I heard on the radio that they airlifted a DPS motor officer off the Loop 202," he said.

"I'll call your dad when I get home," I said.

If something serious happened on the road, Doug often called, and we'd go to the hospital to comfort the family. Because of our experience with Ricky's death and finding ways to cope, people felt we were qualified to help them. Since I hadn't heard from him, I figured it wasn't a big deal. I turned the corner onto my street and my cell rang again.

"Mom, DPS is here at your office to get you," said Justin.

Then Doug's sergeant, Karl Goldsmith, got on the phone. "Sharon..."

"Is it Doug?" I said.

"Yeah."

"Is it bad?"

"Yeah. There's been an accident. Where are you?"

"I'm pulling into my driveway."

"Wait there. We'll get you," he said.

I felt leaden and numb. I parked the car, got out, and went into the house. I thought, It'll be cold at the hospital. I was wearing my dirty clothes, and went to the closet. When I opened the door, I stood there, tears streaming down my face. I thought back to the day when

Gifts My Father Gave Me

I got the phone call about Ricky and had to dress quickly, and when I opened the closet door this time, I thought, What can I put on that doesn't have to be ironed? It's astounding the things that jump into your mind when the world is spinning out of control.

This can't be, I thought. I can't do this again. I took out a pair of jeans and a polo shirt and put them on and went to the front door and stepped out on the porch at the moment the squad car pulled up. Doug's former sergeant, Robbie Milam, was the driver, and I sat up front with him. Justin was in the back. As we started out, the dispatcher squawked on the radio.

"Please be advised, this is a 963A..."

Robbie reached over and turned the radio down. He didn't know if I knew what that meant.

I knew.

"Should I call my parents," I asked Robbie, "or should I call my preacher?"

"Call them all," he said.

I phoned our pastor's number and reached his answering machine. "Ron, this is Sharon, please call me, I need to talk to you as soon as possible." That's all I said.

As we neared the hospital, Robbie called his wife and, like me, was having a hard time saying the words. "Remember to pray for Sharon..." he said. And as an afterthought, he added "...and Doug, too."

That's because he knew.

Then he got a call on his cell phone from the lieutenant who was at the hospital. "We've turned down Roosevelt..." said Robbie.

He hung up and said, "Sharon, when we get there, put your head down. Don't open the doors until the officers come to get you. There are helicopters, media vans, and reporters everywhere."

Doug

When we pulled into the driveway of the county hospital off 24th Street, a sea of tan uniforms surrounded the car. I turned to Justin and said, "You know that dad's dead or they wouldn't do this."

"Shut up!" he said, and flung open the door, jumped out, and slammed his fist on the back door window. He pushed into the crowd and disappeared.

I got out of the car, and put my head down as officers escorted me through the emergency room door. Someone said, "We have a room over here for you."

I thought, I know where the stupid room is. I know why they want me in that room, that miserable room where the relatives of the dead congregate. This was the same hospital where they brought Ricky, and it was the same room I waited in for news of Ricky.

As I turned to go in, Doug's supervisor, Lieutenant Gary Zimmerman, pushed through the crowd of uniforms and said, "I'm sorry, Sharon, Doug didn't make it. He's dead."

I was too shocked to say anything or even ask how it happened. Did it matter?

I began to cry, but knew I had things to do. I had to make phone calls, and it was like swimming underwater, everything slow-moving and agonizing. First, I phoned Misty's office and asked for her supervisor.

"This is Misty's mom. Could you do me a favor? She needs to come to Maricopa County Hospital, but I don't want her to drive. Could somebody bring her?"

"Sure," she said, "what's wrong?"

"Her dad's been in an accident."

I didn't know where Justin was. He probably knew about his father, but I had to tell him for sure. I tried to reach my dad, but he wasn't there. I told my mom, and then I called my sister Gaile.

"Doug's dead," I told her, and she said, "I already know. I'm busy." And she hung up on me. Later I found out she had not recognized my voice choked with tears. She was focused on trying to find my dad.

Our pastor when we moved to Arizona was Lee Steele, and he knew Doug's parents well. He'd moved eight miles from where they lived in Bethany, Oklahoma. I phoned him and asked if he would go over to Doug's parents' house and tell them. I didn't want them to be by themselves when they heard the news, and he was kind enough to do it.

After the phone calls, I asked if I could see Doug, and they led me to the back room, the same room where I saw Ricky. Justin was there, standing alone, looking at his dad. He put his arms around me and we cried.

Then I turned to Doug, and clutched his hand and lay my head on his chest. I sobbed, and Justin held me.

"We've got to find Misty," I whispered.

Justin left the room to see if she had arrived. I turned around and Dave Platt, Doug's best friend, was sitting there. He'd been there the entire time, I didn't even notice. We didn't talk, we just cried. I'll never forget that he stayed with Doug until the coroner came for his body.

Misty finally arrived at the hospital emergency entrance and Justin met her outside and gave her the news. I continued making phone calls, there were too many people to call. The waiting room was crowded with DPS officers, friends, and people from our church. I couldn't walk a step without somebody hugging me and crying.

Nancy Keil, a friend and neighbor, was the director of Messenger's Funeral Home, and on Valentine's Day Doug stopped in and said, "Hey, Nancy, I forgot to get Sharon some flowers. Got any leftovers today?"

"Doug, you can't come in here like this," she said. But he was so funny, she gave him some flowers, I think to get rid of him.

Doug

I phoned her, not for flowers, but because I wanted friends taking care of Doug. The receptionist said she was gone for the day. I said Doug was at Maricopa County Hospital, he had to go to the coroner's, and I wanted the funeral home to pick him up. As it turned out, all I had to do was tell the coroner and he made the arrangements.

I went back to spend time with Doug, and after the coroner moved him out, Jeff Trapp, a DPS officer and longtime friend, drove us home. On the way, I saw our music minister driving in the opposite direction in his van. "There's Bill Abbott," I said to Jeff. "I've got to talk to him."

Jeff flipped on his flashing lights and chased the van. Poor Bill, he thought he was getting pulled over by the police. Instead of a cop, I stepped out of the car and Bill, flabbergasted, rolled down his window. I told him about Doug, and said, "Can the band play at the funeral?"

Bill blanched, and said, "We'll do whatever you want..."

He knew I was acting psychotic. Can you picture some crazy woman chasing you down in a police car? I got back in the car, and as we approached my house, we came upon a roadblock of police cars. Because of the media interest, the police had closed the street at both ends, with guards posted.

By evening, our house was packed with friends and family. Justin had a hard time being around me, I was crying so much. He stayed at a friend's and kept calling and asking, "Is my mom okay?" And then he'd come over. Everyone in the house would be crying, and he'd leave again. He couldn't handle the raw emotions.

My sisters and parents arrived that night. Doug's brother Miles came in the next day, Doug's parents, sisters, and brother Paul arrived two days later, and most of the other relatives over the next few days. Doug's family was shattered. His mother was as if in a trance.

Doug's brothers looked a lot like Doug. It was eerie. When you saw Paul from behind in his boots and jeans, you'd swear it was Doug, but Miles' face looked the most like Doug's.

A couple summers after Doug's death, Misty and I went to a family reunion and Paul walked in wearing a flat top. During the summers it was intolerably hot on the motors and Doug had his hair cut short like that. Paul's resemblance to Doug scared us both, and we were so overcome with sorrow, we had to leave.

Chapter 25

A Man At The Door

We had house guests and I threw clothes in the washer, and then in the dryer. I took the clothes out of the dryer and folded them. Some of the clothes were Doug's and I opened the dresser drawer in the bedroom to put his underwear away. Then I asked myself, Why am I folding his clothes? Why am I putting them away?

I went to the kitchen and got some trash bags, went back to the bedroom, opened the drawers, and began stuffing his clothes in the bags.

"What are you doing?" my mom said.

"I'm throwing Doug's underwear away," I said.

"You can't do that."

"Why can't I?"

She left the room and brought my father in. My dad wrapped his arms around me, and said, "Hun, what are you doing?"

"He's never going to wear them."

"Is this something you must do tonight?"

"Yes," I said.

"Okay," he said, and turned to my mom, and they went into the other room.

My baby sister Gaile appointed herself my guardian. She's five years younger than me, and when we were

Gifts My Father Gave Me

kids, she promised that when I got married, she'd run away from home and live with me. Gaile, like Ande, could do anything. She juggled, rode a unicycle, and was utterly fearless. She grew up into a beautiful woman with dark brown, almost black hair, and looks the most like mom.

She stayed by my side all night, and watched over me. She didn't want me to be alone for a moment. I lay down on the bed. I didn't think I could possibly sleep, but I was exhausted, and dozed off. After I woke up, Gaile said that Justin had been there. He'd come home, pulled up a chair beside my bed, held my hand for two hours, and cried.

The day before, I'd started taking down the Christmas tree, and laying the ornaments on an air hockey table in the family room. I was going to box them up later. Some of the Christmas stuff was from my cow collection. I have cows all over the house—pottery cows, clocks with cow faces, china cows, and even cow figurines. I'd put red bows on some of the cows and hung others on the tree.

Late that night, people asked if they could help with something. I pointed to the Christmas things and they sprang into action. They stuffed the ornaments in sacks and began scattering cows all over the house. In between bouts of crying, I yelled at them, "That cow doesn't go there. This one goes in the other room, not this room," and I'd go into the other room and say, "That cow shouldn't be there, it goes on the shelf over there..."

I was irrational. How were they supposed to know where to put them? Then I picked up the phone and dialed the number for Carrie, the girl who cleaned my house. She knew about Doug and had visited earlier in the day. She answered and sounded drowsy. It was twelve-thirty in the morning, and she'd probably been asleep.

"Can you come over?" I said. "They're putting my cows in the wrong places."

"What?"

"It's Sharon. Can you come to the house? They don't know where to put the cows."

"Can I do it in the morning?"

"What time?" I said.

"About eight."

I hung up and said, "Don't touch anything. Carrie's coming over."

The next morning, she arrived early. Somebody asked her who she was, and she replied, "I'm here to put the cows away." Under other circumstances that would have been funny.

That same morning, the first morning after Doug was killed, I woke up bleary-eyed and depressed and stepped out of bed in my bare feet into a large puddle of water. The laundry room was in my bathroom and during the night a pipe in my washing machine had ruptured, and water poured into my bedroom. I had to slosh through water to get into the living room where people had already started to assemble.

This was in addition to a pipe that had burst in the kitchen wall a couple of weeks before and ruined our wood floors. A plumber had knocked a hole in the wall and fixed the pipe, but we didn't want construction mess during Christmas, and covered the hole with a piece of carpet to keep animals out of the house.

Just as I wondered whether I was losing my mind, there was a knock at the door, and a man I didn't know asked for me. He said how sorry he was about Doug, that he represented a charitable group called the *100 Club*, and their purpose was to help families of police officers and firefighters in times of need. He thanked me for the sacrifice my family had made, and handed me a check for $4,000. He said the money would not bring

Gifts My Father Gave Me

Doug back, but he hoped it would relieve some of the immediate financial burden.

My husband had been killed, I had a house full of people, dirty clothes piled up everywhere, a broken washing machine, a pool of water on the bedroom floor, a hole in the kitchen wall, and out of nowhere a man came to the door and gave me a check. I was deeply touched.

I asked my dad how much a new washing machine cost and he said about $300 to $400. I handed him the check and said, "Buy me a new one, and a dryer, too." I'd never had a matching set before. And even today when I use them, I remember the kindness of strangers. Those machines are my memory stone, a reminder that the community cares.

The caring didn't end there. Within a couple of hours, men from the church appeared and patched the kitchen wall. They started pulling the sinks out of the bathrooms and I said, "What are you doing?"

"We don't want you to worry about drippy faucets because Doug's not here to fix them," one of them said.

Like Doug would have ever fixed them. I lived with leaky faucets for twelve years, and then... those magnificent men replaced the old sinks with new ones. Of all days, though, why today? I guess, why not? Everybody has a need to do something useful, and I was grateful for their help. And I was grateful for everyone else, too. People brought food, and even lugged in another refrigerator to handle it all. People filled the house all day, and the phone rang constantly.

My mom answered one of the calls, and it was somebody named Christine. Then I remembered I had made a hair appointment that morning. I got on the phone and confirmed my appointment. I told her about Doug and that I might not be in good shape. She asked if I wanted to cancel, and I said getting my hair done would make me feel a little better.

A Man At The Door

I went outside to my car, and my sister-in-law said, "You made an appointment to get your hair done?" I told her I made the appointment two weeks ago. She thought I was concerned about how my hair looked. I wasn't. I wanted to do something normal.

Chapter 26

Doug's Squad

After I returned from the hairdresser, the house was still full of people, but I wondered why I hadn't seen anybody from Doug's squad. I was worried about how they were taking his death, and asked Gary Zimmerman, Doug's lieutenant, where they were.

"They can't see you right now," he said.

"Please, tell them I want to see them," I said.

The next day, Sunday, they came to the house to discuss the funeral, and to choose the pallbearers. The troopers in Doug's squad were a close-knit group. Doug was the oldest, and at times we acted like their parents, giving them advice on everything from their love life to their spiritual life. The guys felt grief-stricken about Doug. And guilty.

Then I found out why.

On Friday, Troy Titzer, a member of Doug's squad, was out on his motorcycle and passed an abandoned car in the Gore Area on the Scottsdale entrance ramp of the Loop 202. The Gore Area is between the edge of a highway and the edge of a ramp. It's the triangular area where the ramp and highway meet, defined by two wide solid lines painted white. Although not illegal to park on or drive over at that time, it is a hazardous area.

Farther up the road, Troy met up with Doug on his bike. Troy said he had to go back to the Gore Area to get the car out of there.

"I'll get it," said Doug.

It was shift change, and Troy was supposed to go off duty. Doug was coming on. However, Doug was working a special *55 mph detail*, a federal government plan to enforce the speed limit in order to conserve gas, and wasn't even supposed to deal with parked cars.

"Nah, I'll get it," said Troy.

"Aren't you on your way home?"

"Yeah."

"Go on then, I'll get it," said Doug.

Doug turned back to Scottsdale Road, and stopped behind the abandoned car, which was parked at the end or point of the Gore Area, the most dangerous part of a dangerous area.

It was after two o'clock on a bright Friday afternoon with perfect visibility. Doug called a tow truck, and then proceeded to inventory personal effects inside the car, standard procedure. He stood between the car and his bike, its red and blue lights flashing, writing the report.

At the same time, a twenty-two-year-old man in a maroon Chevy pickup truck on his way to a job interview was rushing up the entrance ramp at Scottsdale Road to get on the freeway. There was a line of cars, and he didn't want to wait. He cut across the white lines and shot into the Gore Area at about 40 to 45 miles per hour.

He didn't see Doug.

He hit the bike first, turning it on its side, and then struck Doug, flipping him in the air over the windshield.

On his way home, Troy heard his radio crackle. It was a civilian speaking. He said he was on the entrance ramp of the 202 and an officer had been run over. He was calling on the officer's radio, and they needed help. Troy feared it was Doug.

He sped over, and when he arrived he saw Shawn Brumley, another motor officer, holding Doug who was stretched out in the middle of the road. Shawn was rocking him and crying. Doug was not responding. I understand that several people had attempted CPR. But Doug had three life threatening injuries: a ruptured spleen, a ruptured aorta and a severed spine. He never had a chance.

Troy told me it was his fault for not moving the car himself, and thought I would blame him.

"How many times do you guys help each other out at shift change?" I said. "You always do that. If it had been the other way around, Doug would have been going home and you would be lying in the road. Would your wife have blamed Doug?"

"Of course not," he said.

"Besides, if Doug knew that whoever went after that car was going to get killed, he would have beat every one of you there. If he had had to make a choice, his life or yours, he wouldn't have let you die."

Chapter 27

Day Is Done

DPS Officer Douglas Edward Knutson

Born—November 30, 1954
Died—January 2, 1998
Killed in-the-line-of-duty
Age—43

Arizona Highway Patrol, Badge Number 3818

Gifts My Father Gave Me

- Officer of the Year, District 17,1990
- Officer of the Year, District 7, 1996
- Officer of the Year, District 7, 1997
- Disabled American Veterans
  Distinguished Service Award, 1997
- Law Enforcement Commendation Medal,
  Sons of the American Revolution,
  Palo Verde Chapter, 1997

*T*uesday afternoon, January 6, 1998...

Doug's funeral procession crawled by, yet I can only remember snippets, snapshots, the things that stood out while my mind rattled off a continuous dialogue of *What am I doing here? Who are these people? What is going on?*, denying the events, as if I were an observer and not involved.

Fellow DPS officers—Dave Platt, Shawn Brumley, Brian Swanty, Troy Titzer, Steve Volden and Sgt. Robbie Milam—dragged the gleaming rosewood coffin from the hearse, rested it on a gurney, and wheeled it into the Scottsdale Bible Church, while a seventh officer, Sgt. Karl Goldsmith, followed behind. They wore white gloves, tan motor uniforms, and tall black motor boots—except for Dave, who wore a dress uniform and the flat-brimmed Smokey-the-Bear hat troopers are known for. The other troopers in attendance wore motor helmets or Smokey hats.

More than 2,000 people filed in, including Governor Jane Hull, who said in her eulogy, "We are shocked, we are in pain and our sorrow is overwhelming."

The coffin, draped with the blue, red and yellow Arizona state flag, was positioned at the front. Doug's photograph sat in the middle, his motorcycle helmet and ball cap to the right, his Smokey on the left. Flowers created a backdrop of brilliant whites, yellows, reds, and purples. Nancy had done a good job.

Doug's brother Miles, a pastor, delivered another eulogy, and said, "More than motorcycles and the excitement, he loved the people."

Misty sang a song about her father, which she had recorded the day after Doug was killed. It represented who her father was, and in her heart still is.

Through the words in the song, she described how her father had viewed the world, how he'd found decency in everyone, no matter how terrible their circumstances. She sang about how he'd related to others, that he could empathize and understand their pain and suffering. And she sang about the Day of Judgment, when she would stand before God, and hoped she would be judged for having her father's kindness and heart.

At the end of the song, Misty said, "I love you, Daddy. See you later," and everyone wept.

After the service, the pallbearers carried Doug's coffin outside. Leading the way to the white hearse, a bagpiper played the mournful notes of *Amazing Grace*, and rows of officers from ten states saluted as the coffin glided by.

The pipes wailed and moaned, and the words, though silent, vibrated in your heart...

How sweet the name of Jesus sounds...

The procession of motorcycles and cars to the cemetery was long and slow and glittered in the bright sunlight like a fantasy animal with multi-colored metal links snaking down the road. It was unreal, monstrous, not of this world, yet strangely comforting.

...In a believer's ear.

Gifts My Father Gave Me

When we arrived at Paradise Memorial Garden, I saw white swans in a pond craning their necks, as if wondering what was going on, a fountain spraying up from the pool raining lightly on their curiosity.

He soothes his sorrows, heals his wounds...

Tall desert willows hung low, and green grass, a luxury in Arizona, enchanted the eye, its beauty in direct contrast to the heartbreaking task at hand.

...And drives away his fear.

Following the hearse, a white horse, motor boots turned backwards in the stirrups symbolizing a fallen comrade, clomped along on the road and then up onto the grass. It was led by a mounted officer and followed by a troop of eleven other officers on horseback. Next came 150 motorcycles, their engines grumbling and thwacking, and then hundreds of cars.

The pallbearers slid the coffin, still draped with the state flag, from the hearse, raised it on a gurney and rolled it across the lawn toward the burial site that Doug would share with Ricky.

After more kind words about Doug were spoken, two officers in dark uniforms suspended the flag a few inches above the coffin. They held it there while rows and rows of officers saluted and a 21-gun salute cracked in the cool winter air. Another trooper played *Taps*. Everyone breathed deeply, the bugle cheerless and lonely...

Day is done... safely rest. God is nigh.

When the last notes of *Taps* echoed and were gone, silence descended, but then four helicopters broke the quiet, thundering overhead. After one veered off, only then did the officers fold the flag into a tight triangle.

I sat in the middle of a row of chairs, with Misty and Justin and my mom and dad and Doug's mom and dad.

DPS Director Joe Albo squatted down and handed me the flag, hugged me, and stepped back. I pressed a corner of the flag to my lips and kissed it, closed my eyes and wept because this was the end of the ceremony, and now I had to live without Doug.

See you in a minute, Ricky... The words from two weeks before reverberated in my mind. I wondered if for a split second before the impact he thought of our son, or as he lay dying, our son appeared to guide him into the light.

After the church and the cemetery, and the long snake of motorcycles and cars left, a throng of people and officers gathered at the house. Some stayed, some left, it was a constant coming and going and hugging and tears. Before long, I was alone. Alone with my thoughts and pointless dreams.

How did I get to this deep, dark place? I wondered.

Chapter 28

A Life For A Life

A few months after Doug died, I found out that he might have had an inkling he was going to die. I was giving a speech at the police academy and told the assembled police officers and their family members about Doug's life and death, and noticed an officer and his wife in the audience crying.

Later they introduced themselves to me as John and Cricket Sayers. They had known Doug for some time because he had put carpet down in their house and they'd become friends, and John, who was also a DPS officer, saw Doug frequently. Then Cricket told me about the time her husband and three kids had been seriously injured when a truck ran up onto the sidewalk and hit them. Doug arrived to take her to the hospital. She panicked. Doug told her to take a deep breath, that he was going to pray for her, and he'd stick with her the whole time and she would get through this.

At the hospital, the doctor said everyone was in critical condition, but they didn't know if John would survive. Doug, in full trooper uniform, put his arms around her and said, "Let's pray and ask God to help him." She said, "You'll never know what an impact that had on our lives." John survived, and so did the kids.

Then Cricket told me a startling story. She said that on the Wednesday night a day and a half before Doug died, John had a nightmare. He woke up distraught and said, "Doug's got to get off that motorcycle. I have a feeling he's going to be killed."

John phoned Doug, and on Thursday they met and John described the nightmare. According to John, Doug's response was, "If the Lord's ready for me and I'm on my bike, then that's how I'm going to go."

Doug got home late Thursday night and didn't have a chance to tell me about his talk with John. If he had told me, I'm not sure what I would have said or done, if anything. He wouldn't have gotten off his bike, he wouldn't have quit work. John had a premonition that I can't explain and neither can he. There are things beyond our comprehension.

For instance, how do you explain the assault two weeks earlier? I thought Doug was going to die, and was thankful his life was spared. And then fourteen days later it was taken. Why would God give Doug his life and then take it from him? The morning of the funeral, everything became clear. I could hear God's voice in my head—

—I gave you two extra weeks...

And I understood the assault was not an abhorrent thing after all. It was a blessing. It inspired us during those two weeks to talk about love, life, God and eternity. Doug told me he was ready to meet the Lord. His soul was at peace and he had nothing to regret from his earthly life.

All the same, knowing Doug was ready and at peace didn't make me less angry with God. When Ricky died, I felt that God supported me and made me breathe again.

When Doug died, I felt that God was punishing me. God allowed it to happen, and instead of helping me breathe again, He took my breath away.

I can't blame God for Doug's death. He didn't kill him. A man anxious about a job interview killed him. But after Doug's death, I was broken, and couldn't participate in anything that in the past had brought me joy. For a year I wouldn't sing at church, or teach children, and I told the preacher, "I don't feel up to it."

Sometimes we think others have it easier, that they can cope with their struggles. Don't fool yourself. Grief is the hardest thing you or anyone else will experience in a lifetime. And grieving one time, doesn't mean it'll be easier the second time. It's not. I lost a child and that is one kind of grief, but losing a husband is quite different. Not all grief is the same. It depends on the relationship.

I cannot explain Ricky's death. I can't describe the grief I felt. I was devastated, but that doesn't capture a mother's grief when her child is killed. The words have not been invented that can describe any mother's misery and suffering. I *can* explain losing Doug. It felt like half my heart, half my being had been wrenched from me.

Was one death worst than the other? When Ricky died, Doug and I comforted each other. When I lost Doug, I didn't have my partner, my best friend, my soul mate, to go to. I felt deserted, and lost. But you can't compare the losses. One was as brutal, as horrific as the other.

Ricky's death brought me closer to God. Doug's death created a distance, and I no longer wanted to pray and spend time with my devotions. I didn't want to feel that tugging in my heart.

When Ricky died, I questioned God and said, "Why God? Why did you take him?" But I didn't live there. I didn't dwell on the question or feel betrayed. It didn't own me, invade my every thought or possess me. I believed God was my only hope. It was quite different after Doug died. I wanted an explanation. I wanted to know why this happened, and I wouldn't let it go.

When I lost Ricky, I accepted God's will. When I lost Doug, I refused to accept it. The Lord could've stopped the pickup truck. He created the world. Saving Doug would have been easy for Him.

The year that followed my husband's death became a bitter and unstable time for me. After twenty-four years of marriage, I came home to an empty house, an empty bed, and a night filled with terrors. For a person mentally and spiritually injured like me, nighttime is the enemy. I'd wake in the middle of the night alone, lonely, exhausted from not sleeping, and scared. The house whispered and groaned, and every sound was a fright.

At first, I didn't want to live. Not that I wanted to die, but I didn't want to live a life like this. I'd loved going home and talking about my day and finding out about Doug's day. Without Doug, I had nobody to share my life with. I had nobody that knew me, and understood and loved me the way Doug did. I had no center, no place to walk where my feet touched the ground.

I've always been a people person. I love people coming to my house, taking care of them and making them feel good. I'm always doing things with people, and can't stand being alone. It wasn't that I wanted my kids to move home or wanted a man, I frankly didn't like being alone and single.

With no one to anchor me, I became a wanderer, and got in the car and drove for days by myself. At times I coveted being alone, and other times I craved company. I visited relatives and friends in several states, and didn't want to go home and nobody be there.

When I didn't drive, I flew. Before, I'd call Doug and tell him when I was arriving and he'd pick me up at the airport. Doug loved playing games, and sometimes when I arrived at the airport, he'd hide behind a pillar and run up behind me and scare me. I'd scream and we'd laugh. The first time I flew after Doug was gone, there was nobody to call and nobody to meet me. After I left the plane, I kept looking around, my heart pounding, expecting him to run out and grab me and make me yell. I knew he was dead, yet I had that anticipation.

Sometimes he pulled the same prank when I was shopping. Because he worked late, and I wanted to be up when he came home, I usually went grocery shopping at midnight. I was shopping at Fry's one night, the only customer in the store, picking frozen juices out of the freezer, and all of a sudden somebody seized me from behind. I let out a bloodcurdling scream. It was Doug. Who else would do such a thing? The staff came running to see what atrocious thing had happened, and all they found were two laughing idiots.

He was always acting goofy and doing funny things. He made up songs and sang them to the kids on the way to school in the car. "If I was a little bitty runt, I'd get up and be a grump," and the kids rolled their eyes and laughed.

I remember one of many incidents when he was in the bathtub. He was 6' 2", the tubs are not that long, and his feet were sticking out. He asked me to get his socks. I asked him what for, and he said, "Just give me my socks." I got them, and he put them on his feet, in the bathtub. "When I was growing up," he said, "I wanted to be like Lloyd Bridges in *Sea Hunt*, and wore my socks in the bathtub, and they were my fins." Then he pushed his face under the water and blew bubbles. That was his underwater diver impression.

Gifts My Father Gave Me

I missed him. I missed his nuttiness, and I missed his smile. I missed his complete acceptance of me. He saw me when I was sick, when my hair wasn't combed, when I wasn't wearing makeup, when I wore my grubbiest clothes—and he loved and accepted me at my worst. If other people see you dressed like a street person with your quirks and insecurities, they might not like you. The person who loves you accepts all of you.

Without Doug, I was a ball of pain, the pain from being unhappy and missing my husband. We'd shared everything and I saw myself through his eyes. Without him, I looked in the mirror, and the woman staring back was hollow-eyed.

I was depressed, and sought to alleviate my depression by buying things. After Ricky died, I bought things for Misty and Justin. This time I bought things for myself. I bought clothes, kitchenware, specialty foods, exercise equipment, shoes, and jewelry. As a matter of fact, I bought the same ring and necklace twice, and when I got home, I thought, Gee, I must have really liked them. The truth was my mind was in a fog. I was having trouble remembering things I did.

I understand that buying stuff is common with people who have experienced a life-altering trauma like losing a husband. It makes you feel better, but only for a moment. And now when I visit the widow of a police officer or firefighter, I tell them about the ridiculous things I did, and they laugh because they're doing the same things. It helps them accept that they're normal.

Buying jewelry, in particular, is common with widows. I thought nothing of plunking down a hundred dollars on a ring I liked. I bought more rings than I can wear in a lifetime. I have ten watches and only wear one. Before Doug's death, I would never have thrown money away frivolously. The unfortunate thing is most widows cannot afford to buy this stuff. They often receive government money in a lump sum, which is more money than they've seen in five years, but it goes fast.

Shopping is a coping tool, and not a good one. I said to somebody recently, "If you get the urge to go shopping for jewelry, shop in my bedroom drawer first. I've bought every piece of jewelry you can think of."

Shopping aside, I was a sad, demoralized person after Doug's death. I was adrift in a flat sea, floating aimlessly toward a horizon I could never reach. Nothing had much meaning, and I alternated between crying for days and feeling nothing for days.

Then there was the wall. The shrine I built to Doug, a place where I cried and despaired. Let me explain...

The Christmas before Doug was killed, I surprised him by dedicating a wall in our family room to his career. I had a poster made of him and his motorcycle squad who we called the *tunnel rats*. They patrolled the I-10 and around the tunnel from 7th Street to 7th Avenue in Phoenix. I set up a shelf from which Doug's first aluminum flashlight hung, and put his Ike jacket on it, a pair of worn-out motor boots, and an old motorcycle helmet. I hung a poster of Doug repelling out of a helicopter and another of him shooting his rifle.

With his Officer of the Year awards surrounding everything, the wall looked very impressive, like promotional shots from a Hollywood movie. He told the kids that every morning they were required to bow down to the wall before they could have breakfast. Of course, they didn't.

After Doug's death, the wall became a memorial, a place to honor him, and the media took pictures of it. I used it as a place to weep and mourn, as a shrine, and I noticed that after a few months, I avoided the family room because of the sadness the wall triggered in me. Yet I wasn't ready to take the shrine down. I wasn't ready to let go of him. I wasn't ready to let go of the pain.

Gifts My Father Gave Me

Unhappy, hopeless, I then became involved in a bad relationship. Why, I'm not quite sure. Maybe to break the dullness and sorrow of my days. Maybe because I was a lost soul and thought God had deserted me. I hadn't grasped that it was I who had deserted God.

The relationship lasted several months. I regretted every moment of it, yet could not or would not stop it until it became unbearable. It must have given me something, fulfilled some need. I know it gave me something to do and look forward to. It dragged me out of the mud pit of despair I'd sunk into. But it was wrong. My spirit screamed it was wrong. I'm glad I ended it, and wished it had never started. I guess I was afraid to be alone.

I was never good at being alone, and my fears came to a head about eight months after Doug died. I was taking a shower and went to shave my legs and discovered the razor was dull. Dripping wet, I stepped into the bathroom, slid the old blade out and opened drawer after drawer looking for a new blade. Doug used to buy the blades and razors because I was always buying the wrong blades and we ended up with a dozen packages for razors we didn't have. Doug had to buy new razors just so we could use up the wrong blades.

Finally, I found a few blades in the bottom drawer, and tried to jam them into the razor. None of them fit. I dropped the razor on the sink, stepped back into the shower, and realized that I would have to buy the blades and razors from now on. And I lost it. I started to sob, and sat down in the shower and rested my head on my knees, letting the water cascade over me. Then I lay down on the floor and cried and screamed at the unfairness of it.

After an hour of feeling sorry for myself, and the water getting colder and colder, I looked down the drain, and saw the eternal blackness and thought, If I could only slip down the drain into oblivion, I wouldn't feel pain anymore. Then I thought, But how in the world could I possibly get my body down that pipe? And then quite unexpectedly, I started to howl with laughter at the silliness of what I was thinking. The drain, the blades, the razors... when you're grieving, it's the little things that get you.

I stepped out of the shower, shivering, my lips blue, my skin wrinkled like a new breed of Chinese spaniel, and comprehended the contradiction. In the height of my meltdown, I found humor in my situation, and realized I must be healing. Because you can't laugh like an idiot while lying on the shower floor swallowing cold water and not have an optimistic outlook on life. That, or I should be locked up in the loony bin.

This seemed to be one of the turning points for me. Either I got up on both feet and took control of my life, or circling the drain, and whizzing down the pipe was where I was headed. I chose life.

Everything was not suddenly a laugh and life was easy. Not at all. I had merely taken one more step in the agonizing progression toward creating a new life for me and for Justin and Misty.

I wasn't the only one having a hard time with Doug's death. My children also had a hard time coping. Justin went into a steep depression. Like Doug, he's got piercing blue eyes, a huge heart, great charm, and doesn't like to show his emotions. After Doug died, Justin quit playing the game of life. He applied for jobs and didn't make much of an effort. He felt it was the employers' responsibility to figure out he's a good investment. He didn't want to play politics. He thought, If you don't accept me for who I am, that's your loss.

When he reads this, he's going to kill me. He hates me talking about him. He hates gossip and people judging people. And in this way, he's like me.

Gifts My Father Gave Me

Misty was as distraught about Doug's death as Justin. Then two weeks after he was killed, Misty announced she was pregnant. She was not married. Even though I didn't approve of what she'd done, I felt she needed my acceptance, love and support, and gave them willingly.

The day Sharon Gaile, my first granddaughter, was born, I thought about Doug and what a great grandfather he would have been. I expect he passed out cigars in heaven, and had probably made up a silly song about her birth.

I wondered if my granddaughter's arrival was God's answer to my question, Why Doug? A life for a life? It didn't make sense.

Chapter 29

God's Peace

After Ricky's death, I wanted to meet the person who ran him over. I wanted him to say he was responsible and sorry for his actions. Eventually, he did. The man who killed Doug... I didn't want to see him, I didn't want to talk to him, I didn't want to know he existed. I wanted justice, pure, simple justice.

He claimed he was trying to avoid a car braking in front of him by swerving into the Gore Area, and didn't see Doug until it was too late. Whether he swerved or was impatient doesn't matter. It was his obligation to control the speed of his car. He drove in a reckless manner and killed a human being, but he didn't even get a ticket.

Our family was outraged at the injustice, and Justin and I went to see the county attorney. We wanted to know what he was going to do about it. We got our answer quickly.

"Because the result ended with death doesn't mean it's a chargeable offense," he said.

"How can you run over somebody" I said, "and not pay the consequences? Don't you think there's something wrong with that?"

Gifts My Father Gave Me

The county attorney didn't respond. Maybe he had nothing to say, but Justin had plenty.

"Outside the door, there's a sign that says you can't bring firearms into this building," he said. "If I brought a firearm in here and shot the clock on the wall because I didn't like what time it said, and the bullet went through the wall and killed your secretary on the other side, would I be charged?"

"Yes," said the county attorney.

"What would I be charged with?"

"Illegally discharging a firearm," he said, "and negligent homicide."

"Why? I didn't know she was there."

"You would be negligent."

"I didn't intend to hurt her, just like the guy in the car didn't intend to kill my father."

"That's different," he said.

"Well, you get on the other side of this wall, and tell me what you would like me to do. Should I fire a bullet or drive a car through the wall? If I go through with a car, you're going to be dead. If I shoot, chances are you won't be hit."

"That's the way the law is," he said.

There was no justice for Justin's father. Eventually the Tempe police charged the man with failing to obey a traffic control device and sentenced him to a diversionary program. He did community service. That's what he got for killing a man, my husband, Justin's father, Misty's dad. After the way the system minimized Ricky's death, I wasn't surprised.

Then Workman's Compensation (called Workers' Comp in some states) worked us over on Doug's benefits and gave us a portion of what it should have been. I came to the conclusion that if I persisted with Workman's Comp, I would become bitter. They had already cheated me, cheated my family, but I didn't want them to ruin my life. I had to walk away, which is what they were counting on. Otherwise, they would rape you and leave you for dead. I prayed everyday that the Lord would help me not be bitter.

I fought the state for months about the Gore Area. I didn't want anybody else to die. Eventually the state Legislature passed a law making it illegal to cross the white lines.

Did I forgive the man who killed my husband? I had to, otherwise hatred and anger would have destroyed me. Did the man forgive himself? I don't know. I understand he was sobbing at the scene.

Then, in case I wasn't jaded enough about the justice system, the county attorney called on Thanksgiving, almost a year after Doug was killed. He said they were dropping charges against the guy who assaulted Doug, the same guy who tried to shoot Doug in the head but the gun misfired. The reason he gave was that Doug was a threat to the men who attacked him.

"Doug was alone, unarmed, against six or eight of them," I said. "One pressed a MAC-11 against his head, and Doug was the threat? The guy was an ex-con, and prohibited from owning a firearm. And you let him walk?"

"There's no victim," said the county attorney.

"I'm a victim," I said. "I witnessed it. I was traumatized and had nightmares."

That wasn't enough to convince the county attorney, and he refused to do anything. I wrote a letter to the judge, begging him to take action. He did, sort of. The judge accepted a plea deal, and gave the thug a year in jail.

Which was not good enough.

Outwardly, to those around me, I seemed to be coping quite well. I still went to church and did all the right things. But inside I was bitter. I was angry, and

Gifts My Father Gave Me

blamed everything on God. He took Doug from us, and when I sought justice for his death and for the assault, there was little to find. If I could have screamed loud enough to shake the gates of heaven, I would have.

After Doug died, I'd lost all joy, and spent a year out of sync with God, running from Him and rejecting His help. I didn't understand why God had allowed bad things to happen to us. Why Doug? Why Ricky? Why me? Finally, one morning I woke up and lay in bed thinking, and the answer became clear. I don't know how I missed it. *Why not me?* What makes me so special that catastrophic misfortune can't happen to me twice?

Things occur that are out of our control, and sometimes we suffer from other people's choices. That's a fact of life. Somebody fell asleep at the wheel and killed Ricky. A man too impatient to wait in line killed Doug. Was it God's fault? He gives us free will and tells us how to make the right choices, but sometimes we make the wrong choices, and once I accepted that flawed human beings had caused my pain and sadness, not God, then my anger at God disappeared.

Except releasing my anger against God didn't solve all my problems. I still woke in the morning feeling dread. Then, on my birthday, a year and a couple of months after Doug was killed, I wrote in my Bible:

> *God, I'll be single. I'll go to Africa and be a missionary. I'll do anything if you give me peace in my life.*

Imagine, I was ready to leave for a foreign country and become a missionary if God would give me peace. You'd think as a preacher's daughter I would have known that God grants peace no matter where you are or what you are doing.

Asking for peace is easy. But it requires giving up something—fear, disbelief, cynicism. With Doug's death, I didn't want to accept God's peace. My heart wasn't right, and I didn't want to make it right. I wanted to be angry. Finally, I accepted that Doug was gone. I accepted that Doug was absent from his body and present with the Lord.

And I felt God's peace.

Chapter 30

Unexpected Gifts

*I*t's hard to believe that good can come from suffering, sorrow or losing a loved one. But it is possible. For me, it was a matter of changing perception, of looking at things in a different way so my healing could begin.

Consider the unexpected gifts I received during my ordeals. Because of Doug's affair, Doug and I grew closer. In order to burn the letters, I had to trust God to put forgiveness in my heart. After Ricky died, God helped me go on.

As a result of my loved ones' deaths, I learned to value my other two children more. I learned to value each day I had with them. I learned to do things today, not wait for a tomorrow that may never come. The greatest unexpected gift I received was the certainty that God will get me through anything.

I would not have chosen my losses. Yet I'm thankful for the unexpected gifts my losses have brought to my life. I'm a much better person than I would have been. I'm a better grandma because I know how precious life is. My losses have brought me close to people I'd never met before. Piles of cards came in the mail from people who heard about Doug. They went out of their way and bought a card and wrote something touching and mailed it. Some of them enclosed checks. The police, people from my church, friends and relatives came to the house and gave me their time and love.

And how do you repay the generosity of those who belong to the 100 Club? I mentioned earlier that I bought a new badly needed washer and dryer with the check they gave me, but I spent most of it on Doug's headstone. That stone is a tribute to Doug's dedication and my family's sacrifice. It is also a testament to the goodness of an organization of anonymous people who show their caring for others.

When Doug died, my family's world stopped, and many people stopped with us. They had families, and jobs, and vacations and things to do, but they made us their priority, and for that I will never forget their kindness. Their names are carved deeply into the walls of my heart.

All told, I received about $22,000 from complete strangers, and I saw this money and Doug's pension as a way to help not only my family, but also as a means to help others. This is one of God's unfathomable gifts. From my despair comes hope for others.

For years, when I've seen someone struggling, sometimes I would pay one of their bills or stick money in their purse or pocket. I'd buy them groceries or take them away for a weekend at my expense. It's God's money and I want to use it for the good He intended.

Recently, a couple of women had to go to Chile on a mission trip. They were to help build a school and work in the orphanage, but the church didn't have the funds to pay for their flights. I put a check in the offering for their airfares. I can't go, but I can be a part of God's work.

I could be a lot poorer because of my losses, but God allowed me to become enriched. I don't mean with money, with His real *wealth*—faith, hope, generosity, compassion, kindness, peace, joy, love, and forgiveness—which it is my responsibility and privilege to offer to those who need them. I'm not a saint, far from it. I'm simply doing what God wants me to do.

Shortly after Doug was killed, the 100 Club asked me to speak at their March banquet. After they introduced me, 350 people stood up and applauded. I was moved, and that evening I talked about hope, and how it helps us survive and blossom.

The most surprising thing that happened as a result of Doug's death, which gives me more confidence in redemption, was that I received a huge plant from Cole Sorenson, the man who ran over Ricky. Apparently, he called our church, spoke to our pastor and asked if he thought I'd be offended if he sent a plant. The pastor told him to go ahead, and a few hours after Doug was killed the plant arrived at our house. Then Cole sent me a letter, and in it he asked how grief and pain could find such good people again.

I cried when I read it and wrote him back. We had breakfast and talked about what it was like for Justin, Misty, and me now that Doug was gone. He said he wasn't worthy to sit at a table with me. That's unquestionably not true. We are all God's children.

Two months after Doug was killed, Misty got married and Cole came to the wedding. It was Misty's idea to invite him. Cole's wife, mother, and father also attended the occasion. I had forgiven Cole and his father, but I don't know that I would have thought about asking them to the wedding. I guess that was the special gift God gave us as a result of Doug's death: forgiveness with grace, kindness and compassion.

In a way, the wedding brought Ricky and Doug closer to us all.

Chapter 31

Love, Again

*T*his book ends with a love story...

Doug's academy drill sergeant, David Felix, attended the funeral, and about six months after Doug died, I gave a talk at DPS. David came up afterwards and introduced himself. He was square-faced, and brushed his short graying hair straight back. He wore thick glasses with small metal frames. I noticed how pretty his eyes were. They were hazel and glittered like tinsel on a tree.

"Oh, you're the guy who yelled at Doug for sixteen weeks," I said. "I know who you are."

We both laughed.

"You never live that down," he said, laugh lines forming around his eyes and mouth. Drill instructors are feared, hated, and loved, and never forgotten.

"I met you before," I said.

"Really? We met?"

"You don't remember?"

I was giving him a hard time. I reminded him it was at Doug's academy graduation. Then David told me about the last time he'd talked to Doug. It was at a DPS Christmas party. I was away speaking at a women's retreat, and Doug was alone. David said he and Doug were standing in the middle of the large dining area, and Doug told him he'd gone back to motors, even though people said he shouldn't. Doug said how happy he was, how much he loved it.

David said he'd never been to a funeral like Doug's before and didn't appreciate fully until then what a joyful person Doug had been, how helpful he was to others, and that he followed his Christian faith. He said Doug was different than other people, and the funeral was all about Doug's love for his Lord.

David said he was proud of having trained guys like Doug who were happy and successful. Everyone respected Doug, and David was especially proud of Doug being named Officer of the Year three times. (After Doug had died, I accepted the third award on his behalf).

We talked a while longer and then said goodbye. Several months later, in 1999, David ran into Doug's academy roommate, Dave Platt. David's wife had left him, it was his second marriage, and he told Doug's best friend that he hated living alone and going home to an empty house. Dave Platt's face brightened with an idea. "You... should give Sharon Knutson a call."

David's response, from what I was told, was, "Oh, no! She's way too good for me. She's the widow of a police hero."

"I didn't say go register at Dillard's Department Store," Dave said, "just take her to dinner and a movie. By the way, she hates to hear that widow-of-police-hero stuff."

Against his better judgment, David decided to call. Dave had informed him I was out of town, and David thought he could leave a message on my voice mail and not have to talk to me.

"Hello," I answered.

"Ahhhhh...Ahhhhh... Sharon?" I heard in the receiver.

"Yeah."

"Are you at home?"

"No, I'm in Michigan."

"How does that work?" he said.

"Well, you go to the airport, you buy a ticket and get on a plane."

"No, I mean... You have your phone with you?"

"Yeah. It's a cell phone." I'm like, modern technology, hello? I think he was nervous. Really nervous.

"I thought maybe we... I was talking to Dave Platt and I thought maybe you might want to go out to dinner or something. He said I should call and ask you out."

He didn't say I was too good for him. I would have hung up on him if he had. He asked when I'd be back and I didn't know, and he said when I got back, I should call him, and I said Okay, and we said goodbye and hung up. It was a sweet conversation. Reminded me of high school.

I was going to fly back on a Saturday morning, and with me was my one-year-old granddaughter, Sharon Gaile. We were planning on taking a cab home from the airport, and I thought, Why don't I call David and see if he'd like to pick us up. I forgot about the three hour time difference and phoned him at seven in the morning Arizona time.

"Hello..."

"David?" He sounded a little out of it.

"Yeah."

"This is Sharon..."

"Are you back in town?"

"I'm boarding a plane in Detroit right now and I'll be in about 2:15 this afternoon, and was wondering if you'd like to pick me up at the airport."

It was quiet at the other end of the phone.

"Well, I was going golfing..."

Then I heard a noise in the background. "Oh, do you have company?"

Gifts My Father Gave Me

"Yeah."

Suddenly I felt sick, and asked myself why I'd called him. "I'm sorry," I said.

"I was fixing breakfast," he said.

"I'll call you later then," I said, and hung up.

The whole way home I was thinking, I wonder who's over there? I call him at 7 AM and he has company? I didn't know what to think. He called that afternoon, and I told him I was sorry for phoning him that early. He said he was looking after his three grandkids overnight and was making them pancakes when I'd called.

"Sure," I said.

"No, really."

I thought maybe a girlfriend had spent the night. I was embarrassed, and decided to never call him again. Nevertheless, we talked off and on over the next few weeks and met up at DPS Family Education Day, which was a program for police families. I was going to give a speech, and we got to know each other a little over lunch. I did most of the talking. Big surprise.

Then one day I was at the DPS training unit, and he was there, and I asked why everyone was saying "Yes Sir" to him. "Are you the boss or something?"

"I'm the Commander of Training. Do you want to see my office," he said.

Well, I was impressed. A couple of weeks later I called to see how he was. He had the flu or something and hadn't been feeling well.

"Hi, what are you doing?" I said.

"Who is this?" he said.

"Sharon."

"I'm grilling pork chops."

"You've got company?"

"Uh-huh."

"I thought you were sick."

"I am."

Not too sick for company, I thought.

"It's a friend from the office," he said.

"Don't tell him I'm on the phone, it'll be all over the office," I said. If he thought I was seeing David, he couldn't possibly resist telling everyone at DPS. And then I thought, Maybe it wasn't somebody from the office and he really had a girlfriend over, and I was interfering. In which case, I'd blown it again.

"Aren't you going to bring me chicken soup?" he said.

"I don't know you that well," I said. With or without chicken soup, I wasn't going to a single guy's house. Today he reminds me I wouldn't help him even when he was *deathly ill.*

After he got well, I invited him to my house for our first real date, a casual dinner for two. The night before, I had been staring at Doug's wall—the memorial or shrine I'd assembled—and it struck me all at once. If I ever wanted a future, I had to let go of the past. If I ever wanted to be healthy again, I had to let go of the pain. That was the message in the book *Message In A Bottle*, which I had recently read.

I got out some boxes and stayed up all night dismantling the shrine and packed everything away for the kids. One day they would probably want Doug's things in their own homes to help remember their father.

I had become so busy taking down the shrine and then rearranging the furniture to hide where it had been that I had forgotten that David was coming over. Then the phone rang. He was at the drugstore up the street, and he asked did I need anything. I jumped in the shower, and he was at my door ten minutes later. My hair was wet, and I quickly pulled on a shirt and jeans and ran to the door barefoot.

I opened the door and almost the first thing he said was, "Where's the shrine?" He'd heard about it from other officers. I told him I had taken it down. And I felt good. I felt like life had a chance.

Fortunately, I had put ribs in the oven that morning and had made a pasta salad, and while I was in the kitchen putting together our dinner, David checked out my hundreds of cows. "This cow thing is a little overdone, don't you think?" he said.

"That's pretty rude," I said.

"Couldn't you find a few more cows?" he laughed.

A few days later, I visited him at his house. He had Mexican Saltillo clay tile on the floors, and no pictures on the walls.

"A little cold, isn't it?" I said.

"That's pretty rude," he said.

It was obviously love. You don't waste time insulting somebody you don't like.

Anyway, back to our first date... After we ate I suggested we go to a movie that started in about fifteen minutes. He said he'd have to get cash at an ATM. I said never mind, I had money. It was apparent at the age of forty that I'd forgotten some of the finer points of dating, like the guy is supposed to pay. I told him to hold on while I ran a comb through my hair, and put on makeup.

Earlier I'd taken the trash bag out of the kitchen can and tied it in a knot. While I was getting ready, he asked if he could take out the trash.

I heard wedding bells.

I told David months later that from that moment on, he was doomed. A guy who volunteers to take out the trash is off the market. However, we were vastly different people, and I didn't know how it could work. He liked everything simple and sterile, and I liked everything country and warm. We were raised totally opposite. Everybody in my family was a teetotaler, and his family drank as part of their everyday life

David asked if I'd like to meet his parents on Easter Sunday. I was planning on going to church with my kids, and invited him to join us. We went to church, my kids went home, and then David and I drove to his folks' house, which is located on the family farm near Florence, Arizona.

There are six kids in his family and everybody was there, and many were smoking and drinking. It was a different environment than I'd experienced with my family, and I was shocked. We ate and then I helped his mom do the dishes. One of his dad's friends was drunk, and he sidled up to me at the sink, and said, "Hey, you shacking up with David?"

"No," I said.

"Yeaaaah... I bet," he said in a drunken stupor.

He was obnoxious and his wife told him to back off. It was at that point I thought, *Get me out of here!*

In spite of being subjected to this pie-eyed bozo, I thought David's mom was sweet and I liked his brothers and sister. They were just different than what I was used to.

Before David met me, he says he drank a lot every night after work. He didn't drink that much when we were alone, but whenever we went to his parents, he seemed to drink more. He says he is an alcoholic. He was never diagnosed by a doctor, but he knows his drinking was out of hand and controlling him.

Then one day, David said he'd quit drinking. When I asked why, he said because he knew I didn't like it. He told my dad, "Sharon brought God into my life and made me sober."

David's comfortable with me talking about his drinking. He wants people to know. He doesn't want them falling into the traps he fell into.

"You don't even know you have a problem until it gets the best of you," he said.

Gifts My Father Gave Me

David drank because of the people he chose to hang out with, the heavy drinking encouraged by police officers, and how he was taught to deal with stress on the police force. Without God in his life, drinking helped him cope with intense feelings and numb the pain after his failed marriages.

I had had doubts about whether we had a future as a couple, but I'd fallen in love with him, and we got married almost eighteen months after Doug died. When I was in high school, I swore I'd never marry anybody who was divorced. David was divorced twice. I swore I'd never marry anybody who drank. David drank (although I didn't know he had a drinking problem). I swore I'd never marry anybody short. David's 5 foot 8. I'm one inch shorter. I tell people David is a tall man inside.

I also tell them he's my $735 trash man. When I married him I lost the Workman's Compensation benefits I was receiving every month. On that first date when he took out the trash, he won my heart, and ultimately cost me a fortune. (He cost me a fortune, but brought riches to our marriage—his daughters Tina and Jada.)

David's mother visited our place after we were married, and I asked her if she'd like a drink. She said, "Sure, a Bud Light." I said we had Diet Coke, water and lemonade.

"David, you don't have liquor in the house?" she said.

"No," said David.

"What have you done to my son?" she said, laughing.

She didn't know I had asked David not to stock alcohol in the house. I didn't want my kids seeing liquor in the refrigerator or in the cupboard.

You may find it hard to believe that I'd marry someone such a short time after the twenty-four years Doug and I had together. Some may wonder why I'd want to marry anybody at all, ever, after the trauma and loss I had endured. The big question I had to ask myself was, Should I leave myself open to loving again? Because a lot of people shut themselves down after losing their husband or wife.

I didn't want to be crippled emotionally and spiritually the rest of my life. I wanted to love again, I wanted to care for somebody else again. I wanted somebody else to care for me.

For me, healing means taking a chance on loving someone again.

Chapter 32

Made In Heaven

*D*avid came into my life at a time I needed stability. I came into David's life when David needed a lifeline. David told my dad, "Sharon saved my soul."

My dad said, "Sharon can't save anybody. God saved you."

David told me he always wanted God in his life, but didn't know what a relationship with Christ entailed. His was a *Santa Claus* God, around on special occasions or when he needed Him. David didn't understand that loving God involved doing and caring for other people and being used by God for good works.

God has changed David's life, and he has written me the most affectionate letters about that transformation.

The following excerpts from a letter he wrote before we were married make me blush, but if you are to know David as I do, you need a pathway into his heart.

Gifts My Father Gave Me

April 8, 1999

I have the absolute greatest respect for you Sharon... from the first time I really saw you and the first time I really heard you... you touched my heart and my soul with the way you carried yourself and the way you expressed yourself. I wasn't in "awe" as much as I was struck somewhere deep inside me that you were different than anyone I ever knew. Your strength and your beauty emanated from somewhere inside of you. I now know it is the influence of God in your life!

I believe, you have earned your own badge of courage by the way you have conducted yourself throughout your life by facing trials, tribulations, happiness, great sadness—terrible fear, troubles, joy, disappointment, pride in accomplishments—and possessing an insatiable capacity to love.

I will keep your "badge" bright and shiny—with a word of encouragement, with an open heart and mind, with a hug, with a kiss and with a smile when you need it so that the bright reflection of Sharon's badge will serve as a light for others to focus upon in their happy and sad times.

Love, David

I showed my dad the letter, and he said, "You better marry this guy."

When I have to go to a tough meeting or somewhere to speak, sometimes David says, "Let me pray with you before you go." And he'll ask God to give me strength and wisdom, to protect me from hurt, and to help me model His love for everyone I meet. After he's prayed for me, I'm different. I walk into the meeting room and I'm not worried or fretting. I am at peace.

People David works with have noticed a difference in him since God entered his life. He has a tough job, having been promoted to Deputy Director of the Arizona Department of Public Safety, but everyone says he seems happy all the time. When somebody asks him how to handle a difficult problem, David sometimes says he will pray about it, and then offers a solution that is heartfelt and loving. He's a good teacher and applies God's Word to his life at home and to his life at work. See why I married him?

When David and I have a problem, he says, "Let's pray about it."

Sometimes I'll reply, "I don't want to pray about it."

Then he gets me with, "Okay, let's call your dad and ask *him*."

Where have I heard that before?

I respond with, "No, you leave my dad out of this."

"Your dad always says pray about it."

You know, being a Christian doesn't mean you are always going to want to pray or be reasonable. That wouldn't be human. But it gives you strength when you need it to live beyond yourself.

My dad likes David. He often says, "God knows the heart and judges the heart." God knows David's heart, and I trust God's knowledge and my father's wisdom.

Doug's friends have accepted David, and now Doug's friends are his friends. My dad visited recently and when he was leaving he turned to me with moist eyes and said, "I think you're good at picking guys."

After I married David, my grieving for Doug didn't suddenly end. I still had a lot of pain to bear—screaming nightmares of animals attacking Doug, dreams of Ricky being alive. Sleepless nights, tears, panic attacks, and the longing for what I had before. There is a big hole in my life. I still love Doug, and I love David. David is my husband and best friend. That doesn't diminish what Doug and I had. David is a different person. I didn't marry him to replace Doug, I married David because of who and what he is and because I love him with all my heart.

What a lucky person I am to have known two wonderful men, and to have experienced two extraordinary loves. Many of us are fortunate to have one love. To have two in one lifetime is God's gift.

As each day goes by, I don't grieve as much for Doug, but I am not completely healed from the trauma of losing him. I did not suddenly escape the pain by marrying somebody else. Grieving takes its own time, and fears have overlapped into my new life. I'm not a nervous type. I don't sit up nights and worry about things. But the first time David was to go somewhere overnight without me, I had a bad reaction.

He was going golfing in Yuma with guys from work, and I said, "We haven't been together a year, and already you're leaving me."

I thought I'd made a joke, but as the day of his departure grew closer, I kept bugging him about it, and didn't know why. The night before he was to leave, he said, "You're having a hard time with this."

That was all he had to say. I started crying. "I'm sorry," I said through my tears, "I don't want you to leave."

"I'm only going golfing," he said.

"I know."

"I'm not going to go," he said.

"Okay," I said, and felt bad about it.

The next morning, he got up and said he'd tell the guys, and went to work. After he left, I said to myself, What is wrong with me? He can't be my prisoner for the rest of his life. I phoned him at work and asked if he told the guys. He said not yet, and I told him to go.

"I don't like seeing you upset," he said. "I'm not going."

"David, this is something I have to deal with. Besides, if everybody at DPS finds out, they'll think I'm a wimp."

I hung up, packed his bag and a cooler of food, grabbed his golf clubs, got the oil changed in the car, and drove to his office. We switched cars and he took off for Yuma, promising to call.

I went home to a silent house. A house like it was after Doug died. I decided to stay up all night. I thought, If I don't go to sleep, then I won't miss David, and I planned a bunch of activities to occupy my time and keep me awake. By eight, I was asleep. At ten, the phone rang. It was David. He woke me up and I was too tired to talk. After that, I was more or less okay. I still don't like him leaving, but I know it's my problem, my journey to seek healing.

Not surprisingly, the fear of losing someone I love is a powerful force in my life. I'd told friends at DPS that if anything happened to David to send Dave Platt to get me. Because I would lose it and I didn't want anybody else to see me like that.

Within the first year of our marriage, right before Christmas, David had to go to Prescott to teach. He said he'd call on the way back, and left for work. One o'clock in the afternoon came and went and I hadn't heard from him. I wasn't worried. I had to go to the store and buy groceries. His family was coming that night for Christmas dinner.

Three o'clock came and I hadn't heard from him. I was wondering what was keeping him. I was standing in a store and called his cell phone. He didn't answer.

Gifts My Father Gave Me

Then my cell phone rang. I thought it was David. It wasn't. It was Dave Platt.

"Where are you?" he said.

"Why do you want to know? I responded.

"I want to know where you're at?" he said.

"Why?" I said, panicky.

"I need to see you," he said.

"I don't want to see you," I said.

"Where are you?"

"In Target."

"I'll be there in a few minutes."

I pushed my shopping cart to the checkout line and stood there crying. I assumed DPS was sending Dave to get me.

I went to my car and sat there and cried. My hands shook. In my mind, I rehearsed what I would tell my mom and dad. I thought about what would come next—

> *I have to call everybody, again. I am not going to fall apart, I'll be brave. After Dave comes, I'll go home, have a migraine headache, and throw up. I'll have a public funeral...*

Dave pulled up, saw me in the car, and said, "Sharon..."

I stared at the steering wheel.

"What's wrong?" he said.

"What do you want?"

"I owe you some money," he said. "If I told you why I was coming, you'd say wait till after Christmas. I got an overtime check and want to pay you."

He handed me the money. I gawked at it, not comprehending.

"Why are you upset?" he said.

"I thought David was dead and they sent you to get me. He was supposed to call. I called his phone. Nobody answered."

My phone rang. It was David. He said he rode up with a colleague and forgot to take his cell phone out of his car. He'd be home in fifteen minutes. I went home, and when David got in I told him what happened.

"What's with you?" he said.

"I'm damaged," I whispered.

He laughed and tears trickled down his face.

When you're damaged, you don't think rationally. Once something horrific has happened to you, you think it can happen again. Even if you don't live in fear, the vision of what you lived through pops into your head, whether you want it to or not, anytime, any-place. What I think helped trigger my response this time was that it was close to the anniversary date of Doug's death, and traumatized people often relive their worst experiences near or on the date it happened.

To help with my healing, after Doug died I joined a police family support group called *Concerns of Police Survivors (COPS)*. It allowed me to talk about my feelings in front of other survivors, people who would understand. Before long, they asked me to be president of the Arizona chapter, and I accepted humbly. It's not an organization you want to be a member of because to join you must have lost someone you loved. I stayed two years, and then received training in crisis intervention, a way I could help others heal.

Then terrorists destroyed the World Trade Center in New York City and attacked the Pentagon, killing more than 3,000 police officers, firefighters and civilians.

I flew to New York with Sarah Hallett, a soft-spoken, gifted police psychologist and police officer from Arizona, and for twenty-four days (Sarah stayed weeks longer) we donated our time to a police peer support organization called *Police Organization Providing Peer Assistance* (P.O.P.P.A.). A police peer support person is a cop trained to help other cops when they are overwhelmed by stress and tragedy. The organization was created by Bill Genêt, a bighearted cop of thirty-two years experience, and former trustee of the Patrolmen's Benevolent Association, who took us under his wing.

While in New York, I was informed that the 100 Club had elected me to their board of directors. Later, the association asked me to become their Executive Director. It was the first time a survivor would represent the nonprofit, and I felt flattered and blessed, and knew I had a monumental job ahead of me.

One of my roles was speaking in public. And I would tell groups of people Doug's story. Poor David. He would read my speech before I delivered it, and then sit in the audience. The speech was all about Doug. You'd think it would bother him after awhile. It never did.

Once before a big speech I said, "Aren't you sick of it? Don't you sit there and think, I'm sick of her talking about Doug?"

"That's who you are," he said. "When I hear you speak, I think, If she can love me as much as she loved him, then I'm lucky."

I married David when I was forty-one. I was a different person than the sixteen-year-old that married Doug. I wasn't looking for the same things in life. David and I chose each other as adults to spend the rest of our lives together, and we accepted everything about each other. Okay, maybe not everything. We're still working on a few things...

When we go out, people often introduce me as Doug's wife, and David's okay with it. As a matter of fact, he's turned it around. We were at a gathering, and instead of somebody else introducing me, David did the honors and said, "Have you met my wife, Sharon Knutson? She was married to Doug."

The mix-up with names occurs not only when we are out together, but sometimes when David has to talk to people on his own. Once he had to call the church for something and the youth pastor answered the phone.

"This is David Felix."

"Do I know you?" the youth pastor said.

"Yeah, you know... David Felix."

"I'm sorry," he replied. "I don't know you."

Exasperated, David said, "Let me introduce myself a different way. This is David Felix-*Knutson*."

"Oh, Dave. I'm sorry..."

Now David introduces himself like that all the time, and makes people feel comfortable about it. He's never been intimidated by my past. He once attended a class at Police Week, which occurs every May in Washington, D.C., and the name of the class was, *Help, I Married the Hero's Widow*. Apparently, marrying the hero's widow is more common than you might think.

David's good at letting me work through my feelings and crying when I have to, and he's cried with me. He's easy to live with and I am very happy, yet there is sadness in my heart. Doug and I had children together and had a different kind of connection. I wish he could see Justin and Misty growing up.

Some people think that if your relationship ended with a lot of pain and suffering then somehow that negates the years of loving and closeness. One has nothing to do with the other. Sometimes I cry, and it's not about the loss, it's about the time we had together. Twenty-four years is a lifetime for many people, and not everyone has good years like Doug and me. We were fortunate. We were given a gift.

Now I'm blessed with another gift—David *Felix*.

Epilogue

Finding Joy After Tragedy

S peaking for the 100 Club is hard on me. I share my story and pain over and over again and it can open the wound. If it helps other people, then I'm willing to do it. The 100 Club survives on donations, and if my speeches convince businesses and individuals to donate to the organization's good causes to help those who are suffering, I'll do it.

My father feels it is a privilege to serve other people, and I feel the same way. When I was a child, he told me, "Whatever you are asked to do, do your best, as if you're doing it for God." That was the higher calling. Serve people, and serve them like you are doing it for God.

If you were to sum up the things I learned as a child and how I try to live my life, it would come down to two principles:

> Love the Lord with all your heart.
> Love your neighbor as yourself.
>
> —Luke 10:27

Gifts My Father Gave Me

They are my whole life. Simple ideas. Hard to accomplish. By helping others, I've found a way to heal.

I hope my words have offered you comfort. I am aware that we each follow our own path and find our own way, and what is right for me may not be right for you.

The Scriptures say truth will set you free and bring you joy. Writing this book has set me free. I feel joy in my heart and know that happiness is peace with God, and only God gives you peace.

I wish you happiness, joy and peace...

happiness, joy, peace

May God's light and love shine upon you and shower you with the gifts my father gave me.

Sharon

Grieving and Healing Guide

*F*inding joy after tragedy is all about healing, and to heal I had to learn about grieving.

As well as having learned from my own grief and loss, I've talked to others who have lost loved ones and read books on the grieving process, and now help others with their grief. I hope that the knowledge I have gained will help you with your loss.

I don't consider myself an expert on the subject as nobody is. Nobody can be. Everyone grieves differently. We can't possibly know how another person will grieve and express such deep emotions. The most any of us can do is to listen and share our own stories of grief, survival, and healing and validate the normal feelings someone who has lost a loved one experiences.

If your loved one has died

I am very sorry for your loss. The following may be what you are feeling right now—

Shock and denial

If your loved one died recently, you are feeling unspeakable pain. You are probably in shock. You think you are going crazy. It is likely your blood pressure has gone up and your heart is pounding. Your mouth is dry. You're feeling dizzy and nauseated. It's hard to catch your breath. You may hyperventilate, and feel like someone has punched you in the stomach. You can't believe this could happen to you, to your family. But as much as you try to deny it, you know it's true.

Anger and fear

You are angry. This can't happen to you. This happens to other people. You are angry at the doctors, at family members, at friends, at God, at the perpetrator if this was the result of a crime, at yourself, and at your loved one for leaving you. We get angry when we're afraid, and you are afraid because now everything has changed. Your hopes and dreams and the way you have lived your life have changed.

Bargaining

"Okay, God," you might say, "you've got my attention. I'll be a better person. I'll help the poor. I'll become a missionary. Anything you want, just tell me it was a mistake and my loved one is still alive. This is just a bad dream, isn't it?"

Sadness and despair

You feel immense sorrow. You feel like you will never be happy again, that you will never stop crying. You can't sleep or if you fall asleep, you have nightmares and wake up in the middle of the night thinking of how your world has ended. You can't eat, or if you do eat, you overeat and eat things you'd never have dreamed of eating before. You think of your loved one constantly. Did he suffer? Was she thinking of me at the end? You miss him and can't see how life can go on.

Anxiety

You are on edge, fearful, nervous. You wonder if something like this could happen again. You worry about your loved ones, their health, their trips away from home. You worry if you will be able to take care of yourself. Every little thing seems to bother you and you get irritable and frustrated. You can't concentrate. You may forget things and become absent-minded because your mind is preoccupied with thoughts of your loved one's death and how your life has changed.

Guilt

You feel guilty about your loved one dying. Why him? Why her? Why not you instead?

Loneliness and emptiness

You feel so alone. There are people around you, but you still feel alone. You feel empty inside, like you have no heart, no mind. You feel numb and frozen inside, like you have been beaten up beyond feeling or caring. You feel like nobody else in the world has felt what you are feeling now because it is too horrible.

Depression

You are depressed. You wake up in the morning and struggle just to put your feet on the floor. Everything is a difficult task. Making a cup of coffee or a piece of toast seems like a monumental job. You can't even think about taking a shower or getting dressed. You just want to lie in bed and die—to stop thinking, to stop hurting. You feel bitter, hopeless and helpless. You feel like your whole mind and body want to shut down.

Confusion

What do you do now? How can you go on? Looking after the bills, the house, the apartment, the kids, or a parent seems overwhelming. The simplest chores seem impossible to accomplish. There is no way you can face going to work. Or you may look at work as your haven, a way to reorganize your life, and then you bury yourself in work. What you also bury is your feelings, feelings that will one day resurface.

Gifts My Father Gave Me

Irritability

You feel irritable. Every little thing bothers you, things that normally wouldn't even merit a comment. If anybody says something to you, you blow up. If somebody asks a question, you tell them to figure it out for themselves. You don't understand how life can go on for them when your life is a mess.

Exhaustion

You are exhausted, more tired than you've ever been. Maybe it's because you can't sleep. Maybe it's because you are sleeping too much. It's because every part of your life has changed and will never be the same. You are experiencing every emotion you've ever felt throughout your life, some emotions you've only heard about—from love to hate, from rage to despair—and you are experiencing them all at once. That's exhausting, wearing you down.

Physical illness

You may get physically ill. Because your immune system has crashed. You may get a cold or the flu, even pneumonia. You may throw up, have headaches, diarrhea, migraine headaches that you've never had before. You may tremble, get backaches, and every muscle and bone in your body feels sore. You don't have any energy. You may have chest pains, and your stomach feels hollow and achy.

Acceptance

After running the full range of feelings and some time has passed, you may wake up one morning and realize that you have accepted your loss. You have accepted that your wife or husband, son or daughter, mother, father, grandparent, friend, colleague has died, and your life must go on. This is the moment when healing begins.

Some people feel all of the emotions, others feel very few, and some feel nothing after a death. No one should think that they have to feel anything at any time. We are all different in the way we experience and express tragedy. If you feel like you are getting physically sick, please see a doctor.

Are there stages of grieving?

You may have heard or read that there are five stages of grief you are supposed to experience, one after the other in sequence. They include denial, anger, bargaining, depression and acceptance. I can tell you from personal experience that this supposition is not true. And recent literature backs me up.

We may experience these stages, but we don't always go through them in order, and there are more than five stages. It depends on the individual. And there is no right order, no right way to grieve. Sometimes we may experience two or three stages at the same time. Sometimes we skip one or two of them. Sometimes we go back and re-experience the stage we've already been in. There are no rules. We are all unique and experience grief in different ways.

For most of us, the possible stages I've just outlined are more likely the feelings we endure to *begin* our grieving. The stages end with acceptance, and until we finally accept that our loved one is gone, we are not ready to grieve fully. Once we have accepted it, then we are ready to grieve.

What is grief?

Then if the stages I've outlined are the beginning of grief, what is grief? Grief is suffering. There is no other way to look at it. And there are no short cuts through it. Grief is experiencing the pain of the emotions and the uncertainty of the future. Grief is trying to seek meaning in the inexplicable. It is missing your loved one and trying to find a way to say goodbye. Grief is also adjusting to living without your loved one, and eventually investing emotionally in others, which is the toughest part of the grieving and healing process.

Grief reactions are normal

Please understand that there is nothing wrong with you mentally. Grief is a natural, normal process, and the reactions we have to losing someone we love are expected and predictable. Because we are human, we react with emotions that seem out of control. We seem out of control as we work through the multitude of feelings. We feel like we are going around in circles, but you are in fact making progress and the healing process is underway.

How long does it take to grieve?

Everyone takes their own time, and no one should be rushed or think they should be "over it" at any particular time. There is no time limit on a certain stage. You shouldn't tick them off on a list as you pass through them, as you may revisit them for unfinished business. A publication I read suggests that if you are still grieving after two months, then you should see a therapist. I think that if you are still grieving to the extent that you can't get out of bed or function after two to four months, perhaps you should seek help.

Do men and women grieve differently?

I read that men and women grieve differently. Men supposedly keep their feelings to themselves. They don't like talking about them, and that's common male behavior. But when it comes to losing a child and expressing emotions, I haven't seen a real difference between men and women. Perhaps men are more demonstrative physically, whereas women cry more. I think the important thing whether you are a man or a woman is to give yourself permission to grieve and express your feelings.

Be patient with yourself

We sometimes feel compelled that we should "get on with things." This isn't one of those things. Instead, you should reduce the things you are presently doing to give yourself the time to grieve properly. Don't take on extra responsibilities. Be patient. Set aside time to grieve. The rest of your life can wait. If you don't grieve, the rest of your life may turn out unhappy.

Be kind to yourself

You are a wonderful, deserving person who is going through a terrible ordeal. We are often harder on ourselves than on others, but this is the time not to think of others, but to think of ourselves and be good to ourselves.

Take a nap when you feel like it, have a hot bath, let others do things for you. Try to eat. Keep up your strength. Eat good, nutritious food, not junk with lots of fat, salt and sugar. Try to sleep. If you can't, see your doctor. Stay away from alcohol. It may relieve anxiety initially, but in the long run it will make things worst.

Exercise. Go for a bike ride, take a walk or a run. Burn off the stress hormones like adrenaline and cortisol that have invaded your body and are making you ache all over. Have a massage, get your hair done, have a facial. Go to a funny movie, make yourself laugh. Reminisce about your loved one, the good things, the happy times. If it comforts you, go to a house of worship. Pray. Cry when you feel like it, but also laugh. Remember the good times.

Put off major decisions

You are overwhelmed and probably confused. Now is not the time to make major decisions. If you have been thinking about separation or divorce, don't use this tragedy as a reason to suddenly announce your intentions or seek out a lawyer. You may feel differently in a few months. Now is not the time to put the house up for sale or quit or change jobs. You've already had a traumatic life-altering event. You don't want to unintentionally create another one.

Forgiveness

It is natural for us to blame ourselves for what has happened. "If I'd been kinder to him," "If I'd had a chance to say I was sorry," "If I'd had a chance to say goodbye," "If I'd said I love you before she went out the door..." These are phrases grieving people say all the time. We always seem to have regrets. But give yourself a break. Don't be so hard on yourself.

If you believe that your deceased loved one can hear you now, talk to them and say what you wished you had said. Or write it in a journal. In any case, forgive yourself for being imperfect. And try to forgive those who have harmed you or perhaps were responsible for your loved one's death. Release your burden so you don't become bitter.

Many of us are conflicted about those we love. Few relationships are perfect. Forgive yourself for feeling bad thoughts in the past, and forgive your loved one for not being perfect.

Write a Letter

Write a letter to your deceased loved one. Say all the things you wish you had said before they died. Tell them what they have meant to you and still mean to you. Say what you've learned from your loved one. Say the things you felt you never could when they were alive. Release everything that is inside you. If it helps you release the feelings, bury the letter in the backyard, or put it in a bottle and set it afloat, or light a match to it and scatter the ashes in the wind. Keep a copy because it might one day help somebody else.

Talk

Many people try to clam up, but that will hurt you more than talking about what happened. Talk about your loved one. Talk about the things you did together, about the things you had planned and can no longer happen. Let your emotions have a voice. Let your pain come out. Don't push your feelings down, don't suppress them. If you bury your feelings, they will not go away. Feelings are never lost. They will surface sometime in the future and may show themselves in reckless or dangerous behaviors. This is not a time to think you must be strong and tell everyone you are okay and keep everything inside.

Not only that, if you don't deal with your emotions now, as hurtful as they seem right now, they could affect you in the future if you should experience even a minor stressful or traumatic incident. If you have to grieve again, as this is the human experience, grieving will be much harder because all the old unresolved feelings will resurface. In other words, grieve now. Don't put it off. Give yourself the time to talk about your feelings. This will help you accept the finality of your loss.

Who should I talk to?

First, you will probably want to talk to family and friends about your loss. Then you may wish to talk to clergy. Even if you don't believe in God, many of the clergy know how to comfort grieving people and are trained in how to allow the grief process to emerge.

If your loss was as a result of a traumatic incident like a car accident, many clergy are trained in recognizing and counseling traumatized people. Ask about their background. You may also wish to see a grief therapist if you feel that your grieving has gone on too long, if you can't seem to get out of your depression, or if you are feeling suicidal.

Let me restate an important point—not everyone responds the same way when they grieve. And many of us know what we need to make us feel better and to give us clarity. The important thing is to ask people to help and to comfort us. Grieving is too hard to do alone. However, you may not need a therapist. Perhaps a peer support counselor or employee assistance counselor or grief support group will be what you need. Grief support groups are readily available. You can find them where you live by checking the Internet, or turning to the phone book or newspaper for resources. Hospitals, funeral homes, hospices and other agencies will also know where you can find grief support groups.

Will I get over my loss?

This is the hardest question to answer as we are all different. But I can say from my tragic experiences that things have gotten better. The cliché that "time heals all" is not true. I can say that time does heal, but it doesn't heal all. I will never be completely healed. I will never forget my losses. I will always miss my son Ricky and husband Doug. I will always remember the pain of losing them. But life got better and I don't miss them as much. That gnawing feeling in my stomach that stopped me from enjoying life went away, and I found joy and happiness again.

You probably don't want to hear right now that you will get past your terrible loss. Not over it, but past it. If *I* could, I think you can too if you keep yourself open to love. Love is the key to my joy. Accept that your life has changed forever, you will never be the same, but you will learn to live with your loved one's death.

Allow yourself not only to grieve and miss the person you loved, but to laugh, love and enjoy life again. Allow yourself to experience not only the feeling of sadness, but all feelings including the feeling of hope. Empower yourself to grieve so that there may be hope and happiness in the end.

Allow yourself to seek a greater meaning. We may differ in our belief system, but I would be remiss if I didn't say again what gives me hope. It comes from my belief in Jesus Christ, and it is from Him that I believe my strength to continue on with life in the face of extreme loss comes. I wish you the happiness that I have found through my faith.

Closure

I'm sure that many of you have heard the word *closure*. It suggests that when you have completed some stage in the grieving process or criminal justice system, then you can close the book on whatever has happened and miraculously move on with your life. It suggests a psychological or emotional resolution, peace, or a time when the grieving person is healed or you are "over it." Closure also suggests that if by a certain time or date you have not achieved that state of being, then something must be wrong with you. The concept of closure is misleading and incorrect. I don't know how the idea ever evolved because it hurts people more than it helps. There is no such thing as closure. There are turning points in your grieving, but that is not closure. Nothing is closure. And there is nothing wrong with you if you don't have closure, whatever it is supposed to be.

Rituals

Rituals can be very important for helping us feel connected to the one who died, and for marking a change in our lives. Rituals also help us to say we're sorry, thank you for something we forgot to thank them for, and for expressing our continued love and remembrance. A funeral and a memorial are rituals. Marking anniversaries and death dates are rituals. Visiting the cemetery and placing flowers on the grave or going to the spot where they lost their lives and saying prayers are rituals.

Other comforting rituals might be exchanging loving stories about the deceased with family and friends on his or her birthday, planting a tree or flowers on their behalf, having a family dinner and leaving an empty chair and plate, writing a letter once a year, traveling to a favorite vacation spot that you shared, reading greeting cards from your loved one that you've saved, inviting common friends over and sharing stories. Almost anything can be made into a positive, healing ritual that will help you move on, yet still honor the person who is gone.

What should family and friends say to you?

Many people feel uncomfortable when talking to someone who has lost a loved one. Mostly because they don't know what to say, they don't know what is expected of them, or they're afraid of saying the wrong thing.

Here are some pointers for family and friends—

Listen

That is your main role. Listen without judging or thinking you have to change them. Be there, spend time and be a presence, a friend. Hold the grieving person's hand. Say how sorry you are. But listen to the grieving person's story. Listen to it again and again, no matter how many times they want to repeat it. You can't take the pain away, but you can witness it and be there for them. You are there to validate their feelings and let them know that they are reacting normally.

Encourage talk
Encourage the grieving person to talk of the person who died, of the life that has changed, of the future, of the past. This is part of the healing process.

Avoid clichés
Phrases like "It was all for the best," "You can have another child," "At least he didn't suffer," "You must get on with your life," are empty phrases that say nothing and may upset the grieving person. What you can say to help the grieving person are phrases like: "I think you are feeling..." "You feel really down right now..." "Tell me about..." and so on. Validate the person's feelings, draw them out, encourage them to talk.

Everything will not be okay
Don't say "everything will be okay..." Everything will not be okay. Things have changed irrevocably.

Things will not get back to normal
Don't say "after things get back to normal..." Things will not get back to normal. *Normal* has changed forever. The grieving person will have to create a *new* normal, a normal that includes and accepts the loss of the loved one.

Blaming God
Not everyone wants to hear about God and heaven right now. The grieving person may blame God and be angry with Him. It's best to wait for cues from the griever to see if he or she wants to talk about God. And then be cautious about how much you want to respond. Let the griever lead you.

Crying

You can cry with the grieving person. Don't hold yourself back. However, don't start wailing and cause a scene. This will not help with the griever's healing.

Talk about your losses

It's okay for you to talk about loved ones you have lost and what you've learned as a result of grieving. Through your story, you wish to demonstrate that life goes on, that life is a journey and their loss is part of that journey. You don't want to actually say, "Life goes on," as that is a cliché and may irritate the person. But your story and the things you did that helped you cope and heal will be appreciated. Remember, your main role is to listen and to encourage the griever to talk. You don't want to monopolize the conversation. The grieving person needs time and space to go through the process. Be aware, however, that some individuals may not want to talk much.

Support groups

Look into support groups in the griever's area and encourage him or her to attend. If the criminal justice system is involved, call Victim Witness Services, if available, and see what they might be able to do financially and emotionally to support the griever.

After the initial shock of the loss and a short time after the funeral, often family members and friends return to their own lives and activities. That's when the griever is left alone and feels isolated, lonely and abandoned. If you can, check in with them and spend more time. Be prepared that the grieving person may say they want to be alone, but then later want company. This fluctuation is normal. You don't have to be there every minute, but when support people are suddenly withdrawn this is another shock to the griever who needs you more than ever.

Sudden loss as a result of trauma

My losses were made worst because my loved ones were taken from me violently, as a result of human error or folly. The suddenness of it shocked me, and the fact that a person killed them, someone who could have controlled the situation, would overwhelm anybody's abilities to cope. If you have lost someone as a result of accident, homicide, natural disaster, or carelessness, your feelings may be compounded, and you may need a therapist or member of the clergy to help you sort out your feelings—especially because people who have lost someone due to a traumatic incident tend to become emotionally numb and want to avoid thinking of what happened, and this can lead to problems later on.

Loss when your loved one was expected to die

When you are anticipating a loved one will die as a result of a long illness, frailty or old age, often you end up grieving twice—the period before the person dies, and then after they die. I read that people who lose loved ones suddenly are more impacted than those who know somebody is going to die and have the time to prepare for it. I don't know how true that is. How do you prepare for loss and grief? You can't. People who are anticipating someone's death experience the process as never-ending. Perhaps after the death there is a brief feeling of relief because the loved one is not suffering anymore, but that doesn't lessen the grief of losing a loved one. And there should be no shame or guilt in feeling that sense of relief. It is normal.

Grieving comes and goes

It is important to realize that grieving is not one continuous painful experience. It comes and goes in intensity. Some days you will feel better and other days will seem impossible to get through.

Grandparent grief

We sometimes forget that the grandparents of a child grieve and suffer the pain of the loss. In addition to the emotions and grieving stages I outlined earlier, they feel helpless and frustrated. For instance, my parents always thought they could fix whatever problem I was having, but this was one they could never fix and they felt helpless. Ricky's death also represented not only the loss of my dreams and aspirations, but theirs, too. Like me, they won't get to baby-sit him, they won't get to see him go to high school and college and get married. They won't get to offer him advice and guidance. And their frustration and anger exacerbated the other emotions they were experiencing.

Often grandparents feel guilty. "Why couldn't it have been me who died?" you'll often hear them say. It's unnatural for their child or grandchild to die before they do. They would gladly exchange places with the child who died. Sometimes they feel anger at God (my father didn't), the doctors, nurses, police officers or paramedics. In my case, my father was angry at the man who ran over Ricky and even talked about having him killed. My father was later so ashamed of his thoughts that he wrote Cole a letter asking for forgiveness. But my dad's thoughts and feelings are typical of grandparents. Their grief is sometimes described as a "double grief"—grief over the grandchild who died and grief because they are witnessing the pain and suffering of their child, and can't do anything about it.

Children's grief

Even though we may shelter our children from the extreme emotions adults often show after a loved one's death, sometimes we forget that children of every age grieve. They react the same way we do, but feel other emotions as well.

Here are some of the other emotions and reactions children and adolescents may experience—

> They may have stomachaches, headaches, and dry mouth, and experience uncontrolled crying. They may have difficulty breathing and be very sensitive to noise. Their school work may decline, and they may blame themselves for the death, feel insecure, have suicidal thoughts, become very fearful and believe things will never get better.

Gifts My Father Gave Me

They may become depressed, have low self esteem, become hostile and defiant, feel abandoned and hopeless. They may feel panicky, and some may feel relief, and then ashamed. They may feel guilty, and even if the cause of the death is obvious, may make something up that implicates them.

At school they may become aggressive, get into fights, spend more time with fellow classmates, become reckless and engage in alcohol, drugs, or sex.

Some may regress to earlier childhood behaviors such as thumb-sucking, hiding behind you, wanting to sleep in their parents' bed, or becoming fearful if a parent has to go out. Others may become possessive of parents or friends, hide objects that once belonged to the deceased or avoid anything that reminds them of their loved one.

They may make up their own ideas about death if adults use clichés or euphemisms and don't address what happened and answer their questions truthfully. Death may be a new experience for children and they may become frightened because they don't know what to expect. It is unlikely they will know much if anything about the grieving process. While considering the age and developmental level of the child, you may have to explain the meaning of death and that it's okay to cry and grieve.

In addition, children may become uncharacteristically angry and explode with emotion. This reflects how frustrated and helpless the child feels. They may ask the same questions over and over again because they can't accept or believe what has happened.

Don't assume children are not thinking about the tragedy if they don't bring it up. They are, and, even if they don't say so, they are looking to you for comfort and safety. It is helpful to tell the child that you feel fearful and sad just like them.

As with adults, it is essential that children talk about the death, and feel that they can come to you at any moment to discuss their questions and thoughts. Often we do not have answers for their questions, but it is okay to say you don't know. Even after years, children may ask the same questions they did when they were younger as they seek to understand what happened from their new developmental level.

> One word of caution when talking to very young children: do not associate sleep and death. Otherwise, they may become afraid of going to sleep or of their loved ones going to sleep.

Ask the children what they think death is. The more you know about what children are thinking, the better you can address misconceptions and head off problems in the future.

Sometimes in the middle of an explanation children will suddenly turn to play and act like they are no longer interested in discussing the subject. They may try to hide their feelings and say everything is fine. It is likely they are overwhelmed emotionally by the information and are coping in the only way they know how. Don't press children to continue, but bring the subject up at another time.

Parents must treat children with care as some may hide suicidal thoughts. However, adults who are grieving must look after themselves by seeking help, otherwise they will not be able to help their children.

An excellent article on how to help children reacting to the death of a loved one is on the Internet. It's called "The Child's Loss: Death, Grief, and Mourning," by Dr. Bruce D. Perry, and Jana Rubenstein, at: www.teacher.scholastic.com/professional/bruceperry/child_loss.htm. See also: www.ChildTrauma.org.

If your loved one died by suicide

Family and friends of someone who has died by suicide react the same way as anyone who has lost someone suddenly as a result of a violent or traumatic incident—with shock, denial, anger, and so on. But the anger may also be directed at the deceased for doing something so destructive not only to themselves but to everyone who knew them. That anger soon turns to guilt, and everyone feels it to a degree. Why couldn't I have helped her? Why didn't he come to me? Why didn't I know she was suffering? Feeling guilty is natural and normal.

Try not to blame yourself. You are not responsible for somebody else taking his or her own life. It's a decision they made, and they usually do it at a time they knew no one could stop them.

For more on coping after a loved one has committed suicide, please see the web site created by Dr. Daniel W. Clark, a clinical psychologist and expert on suicide. The web site is for suicide survivors and for those who think someone may be contemplating suicide. Please go to: www.criticalconcepts.org. The web site also contains a section on biblical suicides and indicates that the Bible does not condemn these acts.

Resources

The following are several resources for people who are grieving for a loved one or friend. Be sure to check out the resources section of their web sites. There are more resources that you may find of value on the Internet, in your local telephone book, or are featured in your local newspaper.

Organizations that typically offer grief and bereavement support are local religious institutions, pastoral counseling centers, hospitals, mental health or social services agencies, funeral homes, hospices, YMCA or similar organizations, and men's and women's support/discussion groups.

Good Grief Resources

This is one of the most complete collections of grief support resources you will find on the Internet. It has everything from articles, books, magazines, and videos to support groups, counselors and camps for kids who have lost loved ones. Go to: www.goodgriefresources.com.

Grief Recovery Online for All Bereaved

GROWW offers a wide variety of grief and bereavement resources including chat rooms with compassionate people. Go to: www.groww.com.

American Association of Retired People

AARP provides a great deal of information about coping with grief and loss as well as support groups, discussion groups and the practical and emotional things to do after losing a loved one. Go to: www.aarp.org/families/grief_loss.

The Compassionate Friends

With more than 600 chapters nationwide, (and chapters in many countries around the world), The Compassionate Friends non-profit offers grief support to families after the death of a child. PO Box 3696, Oak Brook, IL 60522-3696. Phone (630) 990-0010. Toll Free (877) 969-0010. Go to: www.compassionatefriends.org.

Bereaved Parents of the USA

BP/USA offers support, understanding, compassion and hope to bereaved parents, grandparents and siblings after the death of their children, grandchildren or siblings. The organization has chapters in many US states. On the Internet, go to: www.bereavedparentsusa.org.

Dougy Center for Grieving Children

Through their National Center for Grieving Children and Families, the Dougy Center provides support and training locally, nationally and internationally. Their web site offers guidance on how to help a grieving child and teen, and discusses the issues of kids and funerals, and when death impacts your school. PO Box 86852, Portland, OR 97286. Phone: (503) 775-5683. Toll Free: (866) 775-5683. Go to: www.dougy.org.

Survivors of Suicide

This organization helps those who have lost a loved one as a result of suicide to resolve their grief and pain. Go to: www.survivorsofsuicide.com.

Tragedy Assistance Program for Survivors

TAPS, Inc. is a national, non-profit organization serving the families and friends of those who have died while serving in the Armed Forces. Services include a military survivor peer support network, grief counseling referral, caseworker assistance, and crisis information. 1621 Connecticut Avenue, NW, Suite 300, Washington, DC 20009. Phone: (202) 588-8277. Go to: www.taps.org.

Acknowledgments

I could not have written this book without the love and encouragement of my family and friends. Many of you shared in my grief and healing process. I have learned from you and I am the person I am because of who you are and what you've brought to my life. I thank God for each of you.

I thank my husband David for giving me courage, and the emotional and financial support to write my story, most of which occurred before he even knew me.

Even though this book is about the gifts my father gave me, I thank my mom for teaching me so much of what I know. Mom was the glue that held our family together and it was she who prayed for my dad until he gave his heart to the Lord. After he devoted his life to the ministry, she continued to support him with prayer everyday. I love you mom.

Dave Platt is the best friend anyone could have, and his wife Julie has been there beside him the whole way. He is the one who encouraged David to call me, bought flowers for our wedding, and was best man. He has been there for my kids and my grandkids. He kept his word to Doug to take care of his family, and he's now one of David's best friends. He named his son after Doug, accepted Christ after Doug was killed, and has remained faithful.

Several organizations have played a part in my life's journey. For instance, *Concerns of Police Survivors* (COPS) gave me the opportunity to share my experiences with others who have lost loved ones in-the-line-of-duty. COPS is a special club, not one anybody chooses to join, for its membership is too costly.

Another organization that means a great deal to me is the *National Law Enforcement Officers Memorial* in Washington, DC, under the chairmanship of Craig Floyd. Etched on the

Gifts My Father Gave Me

memorial's marble walls are the names of our loved ones so they will be remembered for the ultimate sacrifice they made to serve and protect the citizens of their jurisdiction. The annual *Candlelight Vigil* provides an opportunity to remember year after year the price paid for our safety and well-being.

Then there's the *Arizona Department of Public Safety*. The DPS provided Doug a place to live his dream, and after his death gave our family support and respect—the men and women who make up this organization are a large part of my family.

No one can forget Bill Genêt and the *Police Organization Providing Peer Assistance* (P.O.P.P.A.), a peer support organization made up of many of the New York City Police Department's finest. They allowed me the privilege of working alongside them after the devastation of September 11, 2001.

A very important organization for police officers, firefighters, and other first responders is the *International Critical Incident Stress Foundation* (ICISF). They provided me the training that prepared me to work at Ground Zero.

How can you praise the members of the *100 Club of Arizona* enough? This organization makes a difference in the lives of those who have walked or will walk in my shoes. As its Executive Director, it allows me to give back to the community and to those who supported me in my time of need. While I was writing this book and reliving parts of my life that are extremely painful, my staff supported me and took care of things I couldn't. They are the best. I can't thank them enough—Tammy Wilson, Elena Finelli, Karely Alcantar, Crystal Rebholz, and Ramsey Beckstead.

I owe a debt of gratitude to the *Christian Leaders and Speakers Seminar* (CLASS) for teaching me how to organize and present a speech to any size crowd.

I'd like to honor the late Lt. Mark Brown of the Arizona Department of Public Safety, my friend, and a friend to the families of police survivors. Mark personally tended to the needs of survivors of DPS officers and personally escorted them to the National Police Memorial week in Washington, DC, to honor their loved ones killed in-the-line-of-duty.

I will never forget the love, support and time given to me by Gary and Jill Zimmerman the year following Doug's death.

Acknowledgments

I would like to thank Tom Jonovich, who retired from the Phoenix Police Department. He takes the Bible's commands seriously about taking care of widows and the fatherless. ("Honor widows" 1 Timothy 5:3; "visit the fatherless and widows" James 1:27) Tom has spent untold hours assisting the widows and children of law enforcement officers. He is the founder of the *Professional Advisory Team* (PAT), a non-profit that provides financial, legal and emotional support to the families of public safety who have a serious life-changing event in their lives.

I thank Diane Scherer, the CEO of the *Phoenix Association of Realtors®* (PAR) for mentoring me and helping me to become the executive director of a nonprofit. Among other things, Diane taught me about Robert's Rules of Order, about how to take board meeting minutes, and encouraged me when the job was bigger than I am.

And I thank my pastors Cal Jernigan, Lee Steele, Dave McGarrah, and Ron Sands, who have been faithful in preaching the Word, and who comfort and challenge us in our daily walk.

I am grateful to the members of the *Monte Vista Church* and the *Scottsdale First Church of the Nazarene*. They supported me through the most difficult times in my life. And I appreciate those in the *Central Christian Church of the East Valley*, where David and I serve and partner in ministering.

I love Paul, Katie, Gary, Danny, Louis, Mark and Nancy Felix for accepting me into their family, and Tina and Jada, David's daughters, who share their dad with me.

I thank all the people who spent hours reading the different drafts of the manuscript and for being honest and constructive in their criticism. My family: mom, dad, Ande, Bill, Terrie and Gaile, Justin and Cassie, John and Misty; my *pretend* daughter, Star Lambert; my friends and colleagues: Diane Scherer, Tammy Wilson, Elena Finelli, Sgt. Jim Warriner, Dr. Sarah Hallett, Craig Floyd, Nancy Keil, Danny Dobson, Jerri McGarrah, Dave and Julie Platt, and my best friend, Carol Sands. And I thank psychologist Ellen Kirschman, author of *I Love A Cop* and *I Love A Firefighter*, and Patricia Loder, Executive Director of *The Compassionate Friends*, for reading the manuscript and offering their testimonials.

Gifts My Father Gave Me

In particular, I thank Renae Griggs, a police officer and director of the *National Police Family Violence Prevention Project*, who wrote pages and pages about the manuscript, and offered detailed analysis and advice. I thank counselor and former LAPD detective William H. Martin, LADC, CEAP/SAP, CAS, and Nancy McCuistion, a well-read lover of literature, for their careful reading, insights, and encouragement. And I thank Barbara Rubel, a bereavement specialist and author of *But I Didn't Say Goodbye* and *Death, Dying and Bereavement*, who gave perceptive observations and suggestions for improving the manuscript. Her publication, *Palette of Grief* ™, will be published in 2006.

In preparation for the writing of this book, I was interviewed extensively, and I thank Judi Holm and Misty Snyder for spending many weeks transcribing the audio tapes.

I have to thank Misty and John, and Justin and Cassie for giving me grandchildren to love and spoil. They bring such joy to my life and help me remember that each day counts for eternity. My grandchildren are: Sharon Gaile Snyder, born 10, 4, 1998; Leora Lynn Snyder, born 11, 30, 1999 on Doug's birthday; Johnie Jean Snyder, born 8, 22, 2002; Ricky Louis Snyder, born 6, 27, 2005; Grace Amber Knutson, born 4, 27, 2005.

I thank Off Madison Ave for the awesome experience of helping to design a book cover.

I thank Allen Kates who has kept me on course, and has shared his talent and passion for writing so I could tell my story clearly and express my hope in My Lord and Savior Jesus Christ.

I thank Jean and Betty Knutson for sharing their first-born son with me and for being wonderful grandparents to Ricky, Justin and Misty.

I thank my former husband Doug for the twenty-four years we shared together and for, even in death, giving me respect and honor.

And lastly, I thank God for putting love and peace in my heart, and for giving me the will and ability to share my story with others who have lost loved ones.

About Allen R. Kates

Photo by Baron Erik Spafford

*A*llen R. Kates, MFAW, BCECR, is author of the nationally and internationally acclaimed book *Cop-Shock, Surviving Posttraumatic Stress Disorder (PTSD)*. The book is read in more than nine countries and was the basis for an A&E Television Network documentary.

Allen has written and produced television documentaries and current affairs programs, and has written screenplays, magazine articles and books.

A writing coach and editor, Allen has a Master of Fine Arts (MFAW) degree in writing. He lives in Tucson, Arizona, and shares his life with wildlife artist Sherry Bryant, five cats, two dogs, two love birds, and two pet cows.

As a member of the International Critical Incident Stress Foundation (ICISF), the American Society for Law Enforcement Training (ASLET), and the American Academy of Experts in Traumatic Stress (AAETS), Allen is committed to increasing awareness of traumatic stress and improving intervention with survivors. He is Board Certified in Emergency Crisis Response (BCECR) and listed in the AAETS' National Registry.

For more information about Allen R. Kates, please go to: www.writingpublishing.com

About Sharon Knutson-Felix

S haron Knutson-Felix experienced the deaths of her six-year-old son, and, years later, her police officer husband. In order to share with others how she went through and survived the grief process, endeavored to heal, and found love and joy again, she wrote the book *Gifts My Father Gave Me, Finding Joy After Tragedy*.

Sharon is the Executive Director of the *100 Club of Arizona*, an organization that supports law enforcement and firefighter families in times of need.

She is a certified law enforcement instructor and serves on the state Critical Incident Stress Team. She is past president of the Arizona chapter of *Concerns of Police Survivors (COPS)*, and is recipient of a special recognition award by the United States Attorney of Arizona for victims' support. She received awards from the Arizona Department of Public Safety for her dedication in helping survivors and families of law enforcement, and for her contributions to establishing a Family Education Day.

The New York City Police Commissioner granted her a special award for her unselfish support in helping families in the aftermath of the September 11, 2001, terrorist attack on the World Trade Center.

Sharon has become an advocate for victims' rights and is sought after as a speaker to talk about law enforcement families, the grief and healing process, and to share her testimony of God's sustaining grace and faithfulness.

Sharon is married to David Felix, Deputy Director of the Arizona Department of Public Safety.

Sharon Knutson-Felix

Photo by Scott Schauer

Gifts My Father Gave Me
Finding Joy After Tragedy

BOOK ORDERING

Toll-Free Telephone Orders
In US, call toll-free (888) 436-1402. EMail: holbrookstpress@theriver.com
All other orders, call (520) 616-7643. Fax: (520) 616-7519

Mail Orders
Name _____

Address _____

City _____ State/Province _____ Zip _____

Phone _____ Fax _____

I Would Like To Order

Quantity	Item	Price	Total
	Gifts My Father Gave Me	$16.95 US Funds	
	Subtotal		
	Sales tax AZ residents add 5.6%		
	Shipping & Handling		
	Total in US Funds		

Please do not send cash. Payment in US funds only. Canadian orders may be required to pay GST. Make checks payable to:

Holbrook Street Press
P.O. Box 399, Cortaro, Arizona 85652-0399 USA

Shipping & Handling
US: Priority Mail—$6.50 for 1 book. Please call if ordering more.
Canada: Global Priority Mail—$7.50 for 1 book. For larger orders, please contact us.
Foreign orders: Call, write, fax or e-mail for information.

Please Visit Us On The Internet
http://www.giftsmyfathergaveme.com
E-mail: holbrookstpress@theriver.com